"*Shattering the Muses* shows us the cataclysm of iconoclasm: that those who destroy idols will also destroy civilization, that art needs to be defended from barbarism: but, just as importantly, that art is itself laden with barbarism: that Apollo can, and does, flay Marsyas. Hanshe writes with the ferocity and verve that have made him one of our most provocative contemporary voices, but he has added a conceptual subtlety and a historical insight that make *Shattering the Muses* a moving elegy for the æsthetic complexity our world is on the brink of losing."

— Nicholas Birns, author of *Theory After Theory* and *Contemporary Australian Literature*

"The anguish of the forfeiture, almost perhaps sacrifice," he writes. "Thought is buried; thought is exiled," he writes elsewhere. In a work shot through with images of desolated libraries and assassinated poets, Hanshe offers both a defiant outcry and agonizing elegy for a history of book-burnings & executions. His text is therefore a most powerful chronicle: that is, it immortalizes an ongoing existential conflict between machineries of ideological suppression and the visionaries who stain pages on behalf of a world that annihilates them. Hanshe thus takes his place among a legion of solitary, war-torn writers — Cendrars, Radnóti, Char, de Nerval — whose words stand against the many regimes of order & domination around us. This book is a counter-current to those forces that look to desolate thought. This book honors our kind.

— Jason Mohagheh, author of *The Chaotic Imagination*, *Inflictions: The Writing of Violence in the Middle East*, and *Insurgent, Poet, Mystic, Sectarian*

Don Quixote's adventures began when he sealed & plastered over the door to his library, enclosing his beloved books forever within the center of his ancestral home. On a larger scale, as Ezra Pound noted, culture begins when we have forgotten the book. *Shattering the Muses* explores similar terrain and a similar paradox of creative destruction. Cast between word and silence, memory and forgetting, the reader enters a labyrinthine assemblage of stories, essays, fictions, facts, anecdotes, quotations, and images that imagine a world in which art and literature might end with a bang, not a whimper. Amid the contemporary din and chatter of blogs and comment streams, the book collects and recollects moments in the life of literature — and in the writing lives of Radnóti, Beckett, Char, Celan, Nietzsche, Rimbaud and others — wherein words teeter on the edge of a twofold annihilation, that of the burning of books and of books that burn from within. In either case, as Pound also suggested, the book should be a ball of light in one's hand. *Shattering the Muses* enacts and demonstrates a cry for such a vision of writing.

— Stuart Kendall, tr. of George Bataille's *Inner Experience*, Blanchot's *Lautréamont & Sade*, and other works

As a series of profound meditations & digressions on the entropy of time and life, as well as the menacing realities of terror & fanaticism, *Shattering the Muses* establishes Hanshe as one of the most innovative and boldest authors currently writing in the English language. At once poetic & philosophical, utopic & dystopic, tragic & comic, this work is a veritable hymn to the redemptive power of art and literature. It is a poignant and beautifully conceived work of art that in turns dazzles and disturbs, an antifascist art-work that upholds Nietzsche's promise that one day man may be delivered from the spirit of revenge. Reading Hanshe makes for an extraordinary experience.

—Keith Ansell-Pearson, Professor of Philosophy, University of Warwick

To B♭
et les corbeaux
& for Fulya

SHATTERING THE MUSES

RAINER J. HANSHE

with original images
by Federico Gori

Contra Mundum Press   New York · London · Melbourne

Library of Congress
Cataloguing-in-Publication Data
Hanshe, Rainer J.; Gori, Federico
Shattering the Muses

—1ˢᵗ Contra Mundum Press
Edition
368 pp., 7 x 10 in.

ISBN 9781940625232

   I. Hanshe, Rainer J.
  II. Title.

  III. Gori, Federico.
  IV. Select images.

2017908468

I was the first, by piercing boxwood with holes wide apart, to produce
the music of the aulos. The sound was sublime; but in the water that
reflected my face, I saw my virgin cheeks deformed. "Art is not worth
this to me; farewell, my aulos!" said I, & threw it away; it fell on the
turf of the riverbank. — Ovid, *Fasti*

And so, with a scribe's knife, King Jehoiakim of Judah cuts the edge of the scroll on which Baruch ben Neriah recorded the dictation of Jeremiah and casts it into his brazier, cutting more and more, column by column, whittling words to pieces as if quartering flesh, till the entire scroll is incinerated.

Words aflame, thought aflame, flesh aflame.

And Yahweh roars:

He shall have no one to sit upon the throne, and his corpse shall be cast out to the heat by day and the frost by night. I will punish him, his descendants, & his servants for their iniquity. I will bring on them, on the inhabitants of Jerusalem, & on the people of Judah, all the evils that I told them.

THE JOURNEY OF RENATO NASO begins one late spring in 2012 —
the separation from country, from city, from language, from …
home (can the eternal nomads ever speak of a **(t)koimo-?*), though
Renato cannot foresee the consequences, or that his departure will be
the onset of, in some strange way, unknowingly putting his life in sus-
pension, or living in a state of *eternal between*, and that a rupture, frac-
ture, and shattering will slowly form within him — a thread is being
stretched so taut it will eventually snap like the cut wires of a suspension
bridge, shooting into the air with ferocious violence, like agitated snakes
ricocheting into oblivion.

All of the frames that structure his life come to their natural end, or col-
lapse through his willing them to collapse, while the violent din of New
York, the grating, shrill, screeching noises, the pestiferous scents, the
degradation, the disturbing density of millions of humans congested in
ever-diminishing spaces, reach an excruciating pitch, not to speak of the
swift evisceration of the city's character: its homogenization, its subur-
banization, its usurpation by the avaricious. It is then that, with hardly
a thought and little planning, he leaves for Berlin. Taking with him only
one suitcase of clothes *&* two small suitcases of books, for the first time
in his life, Renato is separated from his library.

At the airport, since he gravely misjudges the weight of his suitcases,
Renato is forced to abandon many of his books. In a state of severe dejec-
tion, with terrible reluctance, he chooses which to leave behind in the ter-
minal, slowly stacking them one atop the other, as if building a tombstone
— *mettre sa forêt à bandon*. It is the onset of some form of disembodiment.

Before entering the security threshold, he turns back toward his pillar to witness it being dismantled by other passengers, with avidity — the image still haunts him. It feels like bits of his liver are being ripped from out his body.

The anguish of this forfeiture, almost perhaps sacrifice, unknowingly precedes a greater forfeiture, a crisis to come, the event of his eclipse.

*　　*　　*　　*　　*

Before having left for Berlin, Renato stores a large number of his books and other belongings at his brother's house. Several days later, a terrible disaster strikes, devastating New York and the surrounding area. His brother's house is flooded with water & sewage, but Renato's books have been preserved, perched as they are on a long butcher's block in a garage, just six inches from devastation.

Retrospectively, leaving moments before such a disaster imbues his journey with a sense of destiny, his having narrowly escaped a terrible event, one that would have suspended his life in a different way, temporarily trapped him in a city he knew he could no longer live in.

*　　*　　*　　*　　*

                    IT   APPEARS
        and with-
        draws,

                              SHINES
                        and PERISHES
                              MANIFESTING
        & concealing
                    as it unremittingly
                        shifts
        be-
        tween
                              APPEARING

            & with-
            drawing

                              EMERGING FROM

                and re-
                ce
                ding
            i
          n
        t
      o
            its enigmatic
                source
                              The VEILING   appearance
                              the PROJECTING   illusion
                              the HO-LOG(OS)-RAPH
                                              The conflictual,
        agonistic tens-
        ion
        of   PHUSIS
                                        The intimate   unity
                                        the drawn   bow: — —
                                        the   AGON

The poet of the Trans-Siberian is wanted by the Gestapo, not only due to his being a war correspondent for the British, but also because, as they believe, but which is not true, he is a Jewish writer of French expression — compound malediction.

Prior to its distribution, the Gestapo confiscates & pulps *Chez l'armée anglaise*, the collected edition of his *Paris-soir* articles for the British Expeditionary Force.

L'homme foudroyé escapes to Aix-en-Provence, to 12 rue Clemenceau, the house of Mme. Duchâteau, the mother of his wife Raymone, who leaves France for South America to tour with Louis Jouvet. Unlike Charlotte Delbo, she will not return to France to join the Resistance.

The Gestapo occupy the poet's apartment in Paris at 12 avenue Montaigne, as well as his house in Tremblay-sur-Mauldre. They ransack both and destroy his entire library, books collected throughout his life, including from during his voyages around the world, as well as all of his papers. This decimation of the word brings about *une éclipse de ma personnalité* —

Not long after his arrival, the day after an eclipse of the moon, a member of the Gestapo is stationed near him, violating women, violating the retreat of a writer.

For many years, this prodigious, one-armed *bourlinguer* does not write — even in the poet of the Trans-Siberian, language goes silent, the blank page a void

Feuersprüche!

Isaac Babel, Henri Barbusse, Ernst Barlach, Walter Benjamin, Ernst Bloch, Bertolt Brecht, Max Brod, Joseph Conrad, Otto Dix, Alfred Döblin, John Dos Passos, Fyodor Dostoyevsky, Theodore Dreiser, Ilya Ehrenburg, Albert Einstein, Friedrich Engels, Lion Feuchtwanger, Marieluise Fleißer, Leonhard Frank, Sigmund Freud, André Gide, Yvan Goll, Maxim Gorki, Oskar Maria Graf, George Grosz, Jaroslav Hašek, Heinrich Heine, Ernest Hemingway, Hermann Hesse, Ödön von Horvath, Victor Hugo, Aldous Huxley, Heinrich Eduard Jacob, James Joyce, Franz Kafka, Georg Kaiser, Erich Kästner, Helen Keller, Alfred Kerr, Egon Kisch, Siegfried Kracauer, Karl Kraus, D.H. Lawrence, Vladimir Lenin, Theodor Lessing, Alexander Lernet-Holenia, Karl Liebknecht, Jack London, Georg Lukács, Rosa Luxemburg, Heinrich Mann, Klaus Mann, Thomas Mann, Ludwig Marcuse, Marsyas, Karl Marx, Vladimir Mayakovsky, Robert Musil, Vladimir Nabokov, Carl von Ossietzky, Erwin Piscator, Alfred Polgar, Erich Maria Remarque, Ludwig Renn, Rainer Maria Rilke, Joachim Ringelnatz, Romain Rolland, Joseph Roth, Nelly Sachs, Felix Salten, Anna Seghers, Arthur Schnitzler, Upton Sinclair, Carl Sternheim, Bertha von Suttner, Ernst Toller, Leo Tolstoy, Leon Trotsky, Kurt Tucholsky, Jakob Wassermann, Frank Wedekind, H.G. Wells, Franz Werfel, Grete Weiskopf, Arnold Zweig, Stefan Zweig, Isaac Babel

Das war ein Vorspiel nur …

Martin Luther's Birthday
1938

5 July 1940

Führer Directive

Adolf Hitler

authorizes the

Einsatzstab Reichsleiter Rosenberg für die Besetzten Gebiete

to confiscate:

1) books;
2) manuscripts from national libraries & archives;
3) important ecclesiastical & Masonic artifacts; +
4) all valuable cultural property belonging to the

Carte
Ethnographique
de
L'Europe

And so, in 213 BC, Emperor Chin Shin Huang Di orders every page of writing in the empire to be burned publicly so as to rewrite history and elect himself the first ever Emperor of Zhongguo.

The Great Wall, the Terracotta Army, the Bonfires.

O Violent Palimpsest.

Beware the Book?

PROHIBITION!

"You shall not make for yourself a graven image, or any likeness of anything that is in heaven above, or that is in the earth beneath, or that is in the water under the earth."

Exodus 20:4

12 SEPTEMBER 1940

                              O-N-E-----TH-READ

          pulls us
        a-gain-ſt
      our-
selves,
but out of fidelity to another, a thread that s t r e t c h e   s
with   e   q   u   a   l   t   e   n   s   i   o   n
                                                  in the op-
                              po-
                        site
            direct-
ion
                                    we push
                                    a-gain-ſt
                                    IT

          Here is the pressure
                  of BEING;
                the *taut-ness*
                  of   life.
          Here is
                  THE THREAD
                whose tensility is teſted
                                                to the moſt ab-
                          sol-
        ute
ex-t---------r--------------e-----------m-----------e------------------------
        s
                An enigmatic,
                eternal wreſtling,
                for that which we wreſtle
a-
gain-ſt
                    is also that
                    without which
                    we would
                    not be —

Despite developing something of a heimat in Berlin, and despite the degree to which Renato flourishes while there, it doesn't prove to be a *(t)koimo- for him. The temper & spirit of the city, which he finds stolid, haunted by a strange, deathly silence (a historical spectre?), doesn't appeal to him, is ultimately too Prussian, its mores echoing through time in the country's social stratifications, its laws, its unspoken codes; in fact, in its patterns of walking, too. In subtle, pervasive ways, he finds it even conformist, just as it lacks elegance & is devoid of architectural beauty. As Otto Dix said, even in 1923: *One soon tires of Berlin; there's nowhere to really call home.*

It is in Berlin that Renato's ceaseless wandering begins, and the city is less a *(t)koimo-, more a portage, a temporary ... *station* ... from which he frequently travels elsewhere. Although, officially, he lives there for two years, he is only present in the city for an entirety of four months. Due to his work (he is the editor of a journal), he travels to other countries, wandering from Berlin to Hungary, Italy, France, Turkey, and elsewhere.

The effect of this wandering & continual placelessness, the loss of absolute solitude, of abandoning every comfort and vestige of home, of being without a room of his own, further distant from his library, will prove to be threatening. He often refers to himself as a cross between a cloud & a jellyfish.

*   *   *   *   *

Two years later, he returns to NYC to close his apartment so as to make a permanent *(t)koimo- in Europe. Since he is unsure about remaining in Germany, he puts the remainder of his belongings in storage, at his brother's house, thereby more definitively separating himself from his library, which may as well be buried, entombed, for it has been dead to him for two years.

No longer is he surrounded by his books, no longer do they stand like totems about him, rising from floor to ceiling & from wall to wall, piled on tables, on the floor, on his desk, overflowing like vines stretching across walls, proliferating unawares as if growing in the night — thought carved into form, the living word, the page imbued with breath, carried into his veins, the absorption of thought, of vision, of sensibility. No. Squared away, concealed, buried in box after box, his library is inert — hoisted into an attic to remain unread, unseen, untouched, the pages gathering dust, perhaps mites, the books imprisoned in darkness, devoid of light, like fish resting below sand at the bottom of an ocean. Or mummies.

*   *   *   *   *

When Renato finally returns to Europe, he decides that he will no longer remain in Berlin, but before finding a new place to live, he has to continue traveling for work, and so he wanders to Czechoslovakia, Spain, and Bosnia, each new destination separating him further & further from his books, further & further from the word, further & further from reading strictly for leisure, further & further from writing. He cannot foresee when he will ever return to New York. Because he can live anywhere, because his work does not tether him to any specific place, the sense of being nothing more than a cloud, some hovering, ephemeral object with no focused destination, intensifies. He has visited so many countries, and so frequently, that he no longer remembers exactly where he had been, and when. The perpetual but unavoidable dislocation from space also affects his memory, and thereby his thinking.

*   *   *   *   *

NOW

Around the world,

    at daybreak,

        in streets & subways,
        on vehicles & buildings,
        in airports & elsewhere,
          paper & electronic billboards

        ARE EVERYWHERE

DISMANTLED & DESTROYED

Those that remain are entirely

When examining the blackened billboards, investigators around the world
find in each of them the same series of three ingrained letters:

RPF

The culprits behind the gesture remain unknown.

And so, because Xianyang is overcrowded and the palaces of the former kings are too small, Qin orders the burning of books, and Chief Justice Li Si humbly proposes that:

All historical records but those of Qin be burned. If anyone who is not a court scholar dares to keep the ancient songs, historical records, or writing of the hundred schools, these should be confiscated and burned by the provincial governor and army commander. Those who in conversation dare to quote the old songs and records should be publicly executed; those who use old precedents to oppose the new order should have their families wiped out; and officers who know of such cases but fail to report them should be punished in the same way. If thirty days after the issuing of this order the owners of these books have still not had them destroyed, they should have their faces tattooed and be condemned to hard labor at the Great Wall. The only books which need not be destroyed are those dealing with medicine, divination, and agriculture. Those who want to study the law can learn it from the officers.

And when the Emperor sanctions the proposal, in protest, some scholars celebrate the necessity of critique, then flee.

Learning of their escape, the Emperor orders the chief counselor to try the other scholars, each of who incriminate one another, and over 460 are sentenced to death, buried alive in the capital. Others are banished to frontier regions.

Beware the book?

The arrival of the night, of a moment past midnight, the tense time of 02:00 in the morning, when an aircraft observes the signals of the maquisards and reduces its altitude to enable the descent by parachute of the school, or let us say, of the *faction des poètes du tympan*.

Their descent, lit by the bright and knowing argentum of the moon, will not be obstructed, even by the breeze, for they are not guided by the cacophonous bang of the war drum, but by the more silent, more mysterious, more delicate pulse of an *inner drum*, of an interior *tympan*, of the silent call.

Listening attentively, hearkening to that which is typically undetected, the poets of the inner tympan tend with adroitness to the near noiseless event, waiting on tenterhooks, stretching the skin of their ears across space-time, hearkening to rhythms, to sensations, to the subtlest of vibrations — not to the violent beat of the war drum, but to the drum of opposition, to sounds as near-mute as the pulse of a heart, to skins which have not yet broken, however taut they are stretched, with extreme pressures & tensions, testing tensility to its threshold. They listen to the *Tympani of the Muses*, who not only struggle against shattering, *but carry shattering within them*, balancing at the near-edge of disaster, at the near-edge of hope, the gate that is of oblivion, of a — potentially — rending paradox.

At the silent moment when the Owl of Minerva spreads its wings, the Tympani of the Muses resound, echoing over precipices, reverberating before the evanescent light of the moon, shimmering like a light that only the blind can see. *Is this also the moment when the Ærendgast of History takes flight?*

Les conditions de l'armistice, dans ce grand Malheur
général qui s'abattait sur le Français, eurent une ac-
tion immédiate sur mon sort particulier et, comme
pour beaucoup d'autres, bouleversèrent ma vie et
fixèrent ma ligne de conduite dans les années qui
allaient suivre.

Having been forced to flee avenue Montaigne, while hiding from
the Gestapo from 1940 to 1944 and living in poverty, the poet who
lost the lower half of his right arm in the First World War is often
at the Mejanes Library in Aix-en-Provence engaging in research
on levitation, as well as other forms of flight, from the natural to
the technological to the mystic, such as the acts of levitation and
flight presumed to have been performed by Joseph de Cupertino,
who the maimed poet proposed be adopted as the patron saint of
French aviators, like his son Remy, an aviator felled from *le ciel* on
26 November 1945.

*

The ERR engage in sanctioned biblioclasms,
stealing 100s of thousands of books from Prague's
Charles University Library and the Rabbinical
Seminary Libraries of Berlin and Breslau.
They bring them to the Theresienstadt Ghetto
to display in Alfred Rosenberg's Museum of the
Extinct Race.

*

Je ne trouve pas de mots. Un œil témoin? une
prise de conscience accusatrice? un automate?
Comment dénommer les ombres dans le noir?
On n'est pas neutre! Le silence n'est pas humain.

In seclusion, out of his
study of flight in all its forms, out of his silence, out of fire, out
of images, out of his *lotissement du ciel*, the word begins to sound
again in Cendrars, who emerges from being eclipsed *&* returns
to the wor(l)d:

Et alors, j'ai pris feu dans ma solitude car écrire c'est se consumer... L'écriture est un incendie qui embrase un grand remue-ménage d'idées et qui fait flamboyer des associations d'images avant de les réduire en braises crépitantes et en cendres retombantes. Mais si la flamme déclenche l'alerte, la spontanéité du feu reste mystérieuse. Car écrire c'est brûler vif, mais c'est aussi renaître de ses cendres.

What is articulated here too is the enigma of the renewal of the word. Its volcanic regeneration is mysterious, but it comes, even after an eclipse such as Cendrars suffered. Will it come with even greater individual and collective eclipses? Or will some be unmitigated and absolute? Will the most adamant silence come, a silence as unbreakable as stone? A stripping away & transformation of skin? The true and total undoing of genesis? Or worse? Will the world be obliterated and we become but animals, *weltarm und weltlos?*

Under the current circumstances my literary attitude can be expressed only by silence.

René Lacôte

And so, St. Constantine issues edicts against the non-Trinitarian Arians and instigates systematic book burning, proclaiming,

If any writing composed by Arius should be found, it should be handed over to the flames, so that not only will the wickedness of his teaching be obliterated, but nothing will be left even to remind anyone of him. And I hereby make a public order, that if someone should be discovered to have hidden a writing composed by Arius, and not to have immediately brought it forward and destroyed it by fire, his penalty shall be death. As soon as he is discovered in this offense, he shall be submitted for capital punishment ....

Beware the Book?

Arbeit Macht Frei

Les dents des femmes sont des objets si charmants …

To Sergei Esenin

I see — your cut-open hand
maddeningly swings
your own bones like a sack

Why increase the number of suicides?
Better to increase the output of ink!

And, as condolences, poetic junk they gave,
unrehashed hangovers from funerals of the past.
Blunted rhymes are shoved in to exorcise your grave —
is that how a poet is to be honored in the end?
A monument for you hasn't yet been cast —
where it is, bronze reverberant or granite grand? —
but there, already, by memory's bars
dedications and memoirs of rubbish stand.

— Mayakovski

27 December 1925

14 April 1930

… not even a tremor's left.

Each time the billboards are rebuilt and papered or illuminated anew, they are again dismantled, destroyed, &

And each time, the same series of three ingrained letters are discovered in them.

One eclipsed, no longer able to write, suffering from *"si longues et de si douloureuses années de silence,"* but reading, studying flight, another writing to retain his sanity: just over 60 km due north of Aix-en-Provence, in the Parc Naturel Régional du Luberon, Samuel Beckett hides out with his wife in Roussillon, a small village punctuated by deserted windmills and red ochre cliffs rife with abandoned quarries: sanctuaries for munitions, asylums for refugees.

During these years of privation & threat, after a long fallow period, Beckett begins writing again on 1 March 1943, continuing to work on *Watt*, which he originally began in Paris in February 1941, before the exposure of Gloria.

*

The struggle against Jewry & Freemasonry continues: 647 crates of books are stolen from The Alliance Israélite Universelle, 243 from the French Rabbinical Seminary.

*

Beckett says that he writes to get away from war and occupation. A means of staying sane, a way to keep his hand in, to sustain the tautness of the thread, spinning out logos like a beam of light.

The difficulty of knowing, the impossibility of knowing, the collapse of Cartesian totality, the recognition of world and man as radically fragmentary. This is not the anachronistic conflict of matter and spirit; it is the violent discord of a kaleidoscopic configuration of physical & psychological forces. *Oui.* But in the midst of wor(l)d terror, in him, in the one seeking a *Literatur des Unworts*, the word does not go silent; the thread does not disintegrate; logos persists, even as he seeks to castigate it, to eviscerate it, to form a Logoclasts League whose aim is to rupture writing, to allow the void to protrude like a hernia. A deliberate pursuit of silence, through the *Unwort*. The naught is more real than nothing. In his agon with the word, it approaches him like no other:

you must say words, as long as there are any, until they find me, until they say me, strange pain, strange sin, you must go on, perhaps it's done already, perhaps they have said me already, perhaps they have carried me to the threshold of my story, before the door that opens on my story, that would surprise me, if it opens, it will be I, it will be the silence, where I am, I don't know, I'll never know, in the silence you don't know, you must go on, I can't go on, I'll go on.

Yet writing *Watt* is not an escape from war & occupation as the Logoclast characterizes it, certainly not in any strict sense, since he is a key figure of the Resistance, one for whom Nazi bullets are marked, constraining him to flee Paris, to abandon his library, to abandon his archive in the midst of global biblioclasms. Father Alesch, German Abwehr agent № 162, exposes his cell, most of its members being deported to Ravensbruck, Mauthausen, Buchenwald. In the name of the Father, the Son, & the Holy Ghost? If the Gestapo were victorious, as they were with the other members of Gloria, *Murphy* would have been Beckett's final book. To exterminate him would have been to exterminate an œuvre, to eviscerate the history of drama, to disembowel literature and alter a century. Is the history of writing not the history of humanity?

In being constrained to flee Paris, in being separated from his library, from an archive around which his words were born, a literary freedom erupts, as over the recent past, the fractured I of a dissolved *cogito* grew more and more eclipsed from English, saw it as a veil in need of rending so as to reach the concealed nothingness, the sole viable form of expression, where skeptical resignation is forever sustained, not as negation, but as the optimal authentic mode of knowledge — the single light before dark matter, the thread of threads.

*

The biblioclasts persist with Cerberitic force:

In Vilna, Dr. Johannes Pohl of the ERR selects 20,000 significant books out of a larger bounty taken from various towns and 100s of synagogues as well as the sale of over 75,000 books as raw material to deliver to a paper-shredding mill.

And then there are the uncounted books, the uncountable books, those destroyed through the extermination of those who would have been writers, and those who were.

*

The Logoclast isn't solely writing though, but collecting information on the movement of German troops which he deciphers, classifies, translates, and types, readying it for microfilm for transport to London via Madame Picabia (sometimes she conceals the data in her underwear), making contacts between Resistance workers and aiding the retrieval, concealment, and delivering of ammunition for destroying railroad yards used to transport German supplies. Sometimes, he leaves grenades on his terrace; sometimes, he plays chess; sometimes, he retrieves arms from the quarries; sometimes, he writes. If writing leads him to silence, it is to an articulated silence, to a condensation of the logos that makes silence more tangible. It is between words, as between notes, that silence becomes ever palpable. Metaphysical and personal structures collapse; the balance between the word and the world is shattered — it is the permutation that demonstrates the breakdown of knowledge. Stretched beyond the threshold of tautness, like a violin string pitched too high, *the thread snaps.*

The void is breached through the disintegration of rationality, which cannot maintain sense. Humanity is incommensurable. Peering out the window at the old wordless world, little sounds come that demand nothing, ordain nothing, explain nothing, propound nothing, and the short necessary night is soon ended. Darkness accumulates, thickens, then suddenly bursts and drowns everything. Writing leads to silence, yet again, it is through the *logos* that the *alogos* is heard. Forget unifying historical chaos, forget clarifying individual chaos, forget anthropomorphosizing the inhuman necessities that provoke chaos. Bring the straws, the flotsam, names, dates, the first and the final dash, not the final animism, but the pure incoherence of times and men and places, the amusing, the laugh, the long silent guffaw of the knowing non-exister!

When the war is over, the man who preferred blackbirds to nightingales eventually returns to Paris where, unlike for *l'homme foudroyé*, most of his books and papers remain intact — they survive the biblioclasm as he survived the *clasm* of his œuvre. Despite completing *Watt* in December of 1944, & luckily retrieving the bulky manuscript from the British War Office when it was confiscated in early 1945 during his journey to Ireland, the word is not received. It is said to be "too wild and unintelligible," not fit for "allocating any of our very limited supply of paper to its production." Others were baffled by it, responding to it with hostility, saying it was "too difficult." "What is it that this Dublin air does to these writers?" The whoresons did not realize it was born of a different air …

After a near-decade of being rejected, *Watt* is finally published in 1953 —
but what is time to one who knows that the *sub specie æternitatis* vision is
what enables one to persist before disaster?

who may tell the tale
of the old man?
weigh absence in a scale?
mete want with a span?
the sum assess
of the world's woes?
nothingness
in words enclose?

It is in words that nothingness is enclosed; it is in
words that silence is enclosed, in words, just as nothingness is enclosed
between each strand of thread, just as space is enclosed between each
vibrating string, matter between dark matter.

Nature As Seen By Sick Minds!

And so, in ancient Syria, Emperor Jovian destroys the Library of
Antioch as an act of vengeance against Julian the Apostate. And on September 11, he declares that those who worship ancestral gods must die,
and on 23 December, two days before the supposed birth of Christ, death
is promised to those who engage in pagan ceremonies, & pagan texts are
set aflame — *libricide*.

Beware the Book?

Beware the Acolytes.

PROHIBITION!

"The poet's products are inferior in comparison to the truth, and he resembles the painter also in associating with an inferior part of the soul, not with the best part. *By rights, therefore, we ought not to admit him into a city which is going to be well governed,* since it is an inferior part of the soul that he arouses & feeds, and by making this strong destroys the rational part. [...] *The imitative poet sets up a bad regime in the soul of each individual, gratifying the senseless part of it…* He is nothing but an image-maker, & he stands far removed from the truth."

Plato, *The Republic*

The *Unzeitgemäße*
the sacrificial animals
who peer into the *okkos* of their epoch,
that beast with shattered vertebræ,
and seek to join it ~*~

Amidst the deafening noise,
they *hear* it cracking;
through the darkness,
they *see* it cracking,

S   H   A   T   T   E   R   I   N   G

they are the fracture itself
the violent caesura
both obstructing *&* suturing the schism

the poets,
the painters,
the thinkers
all the artisans of some *tekne*
juggling the shattered

V   E   R
T   E   (NE) B   R   A   E

of the beast

buoyed *&* broken by time

shattering *&* suturing

out of desolation,
out of destruction,

THEY RISE
        giving blood to construct

                writing with blood
                painting with blood
                thinking with blood

    to overcome & begin anew

                not to cast the aulos to the riverbank
                not to torture the transgressor
                not to tear the strings from the lyre

                but to tie the knot of Innigkeit
                and, like Marsyas,
                        TO UNITE

    Out of blood, a river

                He is our forbear,
                not Athena
                He gave his flesh
                like Prometheus his liver
                He who perished
                in pursuit of the impossible

Birkenau
Block 31

A clandestine library
8 to 10 books
H. G. Wells' *A Short History of the World*
& others
not to speak
of
the memorized books
recited to the children
of the birch forest

Its readers are all exterminated.

Nous sommes à jamais perdus dans le désert de l'éternèbre.

25 September 1940

How can one still write?
I can sense the deep connection that links a writer to his era
as I had never sensed it before.

All the frameworks of thought in which I thought and lived have,
perhaps, been destroyed.

I feel completely insecure when I write.
My thoughts seem to me those of a madman.
It is the world that is mad around me.

But the effect is the same.

The connection between it and me has been destroyed.

Jean Guéhenno

everything was asleep
as if the whole universe
were a vast error

Upon returning to Berlin, whatever Renato cannot contain in a few suitcases, he puts in storage, including a preponderance of newly acquired books. He now has books in storage in two different countries — one immense library, collected over a period of nearly 30 years, & a single, small bookcase, both in boxes, delimited, the primary material of his life, his sole possession, no longer living, ready to hand, no longer like air moving through his lungs, but inert, dead — *reposing tomes*. They do not speak to him from out of the wall, at night, during the day, during moments of insomnia & desolation, during stimulating moments, during moments of heated cogitation, of meditation & intoxication, the ecstasy of thought. *No.* They do not glance at him, they do not stare at him from afar; he does not go to them consciously or unconsciously, nor does he dream in their midst, like a circle of initiates at a ritual, like friends around a fire, like friends gathering before a lightning-struck tree . . . Once, they were as voluble as living companions. Now, they are stones. This separation has affected his memory, his thinking, and his relationship to the word. The discipline to which he wedded himself is falling from his bones.

And there are those lost books, the ones left behind at the airport, the ones he abandoned, the ones of which he is bereft. Books he has not forgotten, books he has still yet to recover, books which to him seem as suspended as himself, as much clouds or jellyfish, like travelers hovering at a transfer point for years, or not knowing that they never did arrive anywhere, and that the place wherein they live is not their true destination, only a way station beyond which they cannot see, as obscured from their sight and as out of reach as Renato's library is from the touch of his hands. *L'obscurité dans laquelle ses livres existent = l'obscurité dans laquelle il existe.* Throughout this time, the sight of books, most particularly when he encounters them in other people's homes, unnerve him.

*　*　*　*　*

The Harrow is beginning to write; when it finishes the first draft of the inscription on the man's back, the layer of cotton wool begins to roll and slowly turns the body over, to give the Harrow fresh space for writing. Meanwhile the raw part that has been written on lies on the cotton wool, which is specially prepared to staunch the bleeding and so makes all ready for a new deepening of the script. Then these teeth at the edge of the Harrow, as the body turns further around, tear the cotton wool away from the wounds, throw it into the pit, and there is more work for the Harrow. So it keeps on writing deeper and deeper for the whole twelve hours. The first six hours the condemned man stays alive almost as before, he suffers only pain. After two hours the felt gag is taken away, for he has no longer strength to scream. Here, into this electrically heated basin at the head of the Bed, some warm rice pap is poured, from which the man, if he feels like it, can take as much as his tongue can lap. Not one of them ever misses the chance. I can remember none, and my experience is extensive. Only about the sixth hour does the man lose all desire to eat. I usually kneel down here at that moment and observe what happens. The man rarely swallows his last mouthful, he only rolls it around his mouth and spits it out into the pit. I have to duck just then or he would spit it in my face. But how quiet he grows at just about the sixth hour! Enlightenment comes to the most dull-witted. It begins around the eyes. From there it radiates. A moment that might tempt one to get under the Harrow oneself. Nothing more happens than that the man begins to understand the inscription, he purses his mouth as if he were listening. You have seen how difficult it is to decipher the script with one's eyes; *but our man deciphers it with his wounds.* To be sure, that is a hard task; he needs six hours to accomplish it. By that time the Harrow has pierced him quite through and casts him into the pit, where he pitches down upon the blood and water and the cotton wool. Then the judgment has been fulfilled, and we, the soldier *&* I, bury him. — Kafka

After being constructed anew yet again, billboards around the world are once more

But this time, letters slowly become visible on them, pulsating intermittently, in different colors:

And so, in AD 367, Athanasius, the Bishop of Alexandria, warns in his Paschal Letter against the use of apocryphal scriptures, an invention of heretics meant to lead astray the simple. *Only kanonizomena texts are acceptable,* & so the canon begins, & so the circumscription of knowledge, & the orthodoxy, & the *bundle* of right texts.

Beware the Book?

Beware the Canon.

CORPSE #12

While *l'homme foudroyé* is eclipsed, no longer able to write, and Beckett
both writes against & deliberately pursues silence, but *through the word*,
Miklós Radnóti is conscripted into forced labor three times, the third
being definitive, as he foresees, or realizes is inevitable, long before the
bullet strikes:

> Even so will I struggle and so will I die;
> still as a sign to posterity
> the fields will preserve my bones.
> "Like in a Bull" (22 August 1933)

        The murder of Lorca three years
later further convinces Radnóti that his fate will be no different. Writing
on 20 July 1936, when Radio Granada announces the outbreak of hostili-
ties in Spain, in "Garden on Istenhegy" Radnóti asks himself what kind
of death will come to him, this time giving it greater specificity:

> And for you, young man! what kind of death?
> Will a bullet come flying, with an insect sound,
> or will a noisy bomb plow into earth,
> so that, your flesh torn, you will fly about?

        In "O Ancient Prisons,"
written one year after his second conscription, Radnóti speaks of how
distant the noble and heroical death of the poet is, noting that he "who
dares to act enters into an empty void," then likens reality to a cracked
pot incapable of retaining its shape, that its rotted shards will shatter like
a storm. *What*, then, he contemplates, *is the fate of the poet…?* He is
a teacher but, like the pot, the poet is also subject to shattering, for all
things, especially humans, shatter.

        On war ground, during the first con-
scription, the poet clears mines, laboring without weapons in hazardous

territory in the Carpathian Mountains. As a Jew, he lives under the threat
that he can be shot at any time with impunity.

*

28 March 1941

> For us it is a matter of special pride to de-
> stroy the Talmudic Academy, which has
> been known as the greatest in Poland ... We
> threw out of the building the great Talmudic
> Library and carted it to market. There we
> set fire to the books. The fire lasted for twenty
> hours. The Jews of Lublin were assembled
> around and cried bitterly. The cries almost si-
> lenced us. Then we summoned a military band,
> and the joyful shouts of the soldiers silenced the
> sounds of Jewish cries.

*

In his "Second Eclogue,"
a dialogue between a poet & a pilot written on 27 April 1941, six months
after his first conscription and two months before the exhumation of Ta-
merlane's skeleton, when answering the pilot's question, "Did you write
again today?" Radnóti speaks of the poet's art as something ingrained,
like the genetically inscribed functions of animals:

*Yes, I wrote. What else
can I do? Poets write, cats wail, dogs howl and small fish coyly scatter their
eggs. I write about everything. I even write for you, so you'll know I'm alive.
I write when the light of the bloodshot moon stumbles among the exploding,
collapsing rows of houses, when terrified parks are torn up, when breathing
stops, when even the sky vomits, and the planes keep coming. They disappear
and then swoop down again, like the roar of madness! I write. What else
can I do?* And a poem is very dangerous, if you only know how sensitive,
how unpredictable even one line is! *You need bravery for all this, you see.
Cats wail, dogs howl, poets write…*

At the end of the poem, the pilot likens himself to a homeless person — when he is in the sky, he wants to return to the earth; when he is on the earth, he wants to return to the sky, where the rhythm of his pain is, he claims, the same as that of the poet. Speaking then of God, the pilot wonders, "who will understand?" then asks the poet if he will write about him. The poet, who speaks not of faith, responds: "If I'm alive. If there's anyone left." Having undergone what he has, having witnessed the abomination of desolation, the poet knows that faith cannot be invoked. Art is the sole saving sorceress.

And in his First Eclogue, Radnóti configures the act of writing as something natural that continues even in the midst of disaster, of knowing oblivion:

(Shepherd:
What about you? can *your* words find any echo in these times?

Poet:
Cannon rumbling? in ashen ruins, with villages orphaned?
Still, I write, and I live in the midst of this mad-dog world, as
lives that oak: it knows that they'll be cutting it down; that
white cross on it signals: tomorrow the tree men will buzz-
saw the region; calmly it waits for that fate, yet it sprouts new
leaves in the meantime.)

During his second conscription, the poet toils in a sugar factory *&*, like sugar, he too will dissolve, or shatter… Could a thread conserve fracturing crystals?

During his third and final conscription, Radnóti is eventually taken to Lager Heidenau, Yugoslavia, where he and others are made to work on a railroad for copper mines. Throughout this time, in the midst of the terror, as one who suffers its monstrosities directly, before a barbed wire sky, when the prime objective of most if not nearly every prisoner of war is to obtain a shard of bread, an extra spoonful of soup, rags to keep warm, *Radnóti continues to write*, in the midst of abominable privations, in the face of monstrous actions, inscribing poems on scraps of paper and in a note-book a Yugoslavian gardener secretly obtains for him. Writing, the word, does not go silent in this poet; it is clearly fundamental to his being, to his health, his sanity, is as intrinsic to him as breathing. Art is not an adorn-ment. A dying breath is a breath & must be breathed.

This entire period is one of dying breaths, of threads that cannot conserve.

7 JULY 1944:

In the 7th Eclogue, Radnóti evinces with terrible clarity and sharpness the conditions in which he and his shaven-headed companions subsist, where, covered in rags, even the power of fantasy is impotent; only the dream that comes in sleep releases the anguished body and sets the cap-tives out for home. But, the poet questions, *does even a fugitive homeland exist*, one unharmed by bombs? Or have they reached the most extreme and exacting form of *Unheimlichness?* The poet also questions whether or not poetry will find a home. Fifty years later, *sans papier*, Ghérasim Luca would proclaim there is no place in this world for poets, and take his last breath on le Pont Mirabeau…

In his eclogue, Radnóti describes how he writes in the dark, in barbed-wire barracks, his hand moving across the page like a near-blind caterpillar. Nonetheless, all of the verses of this period are written in careful, precise, balanced handwriting, even down to caesuras, the tight, controlled measuring of form acting as a bulwark against chaos and degradation, albeit fragile. Captive, the self-described beast among vermin notes with dark irony that although the fleas renew their siege at night, at least the flies have ceased their attacks — abject relief, mordant irony. While the onset of evening leads to the ferocious barbed wire oak fence dissolving in the twilight, it reappears hours later, highlighted by the moon's cold light, which casts the ominous shadows of armed prison guards upon the wall — their presence is palpable even in their distance, a controlling projection invading the sanctuary of sleep.

On the other side stands a population of 180 million, a mixture of races, whose very names are unpronounceable, and whose physique is such that one can shoot them down without pity or compassion. These animals, that torture and ill-treat every prisoner from our side, every wounded man that they come across and do not treat them the way decent soldiers would, you will see for yourself. These people have been welded by the Jews into one religion, one ideology, which is called Bolshevism for the task: now we have Russia, half of Asia, a part of Europe, now we will overwhelm Germany and the whole world.

When you, my men, fight in the east, you are carrying on the same struggle, against the same sub-humanity, the same inferior races, that at one time appeared under the name of Huns, another time — one thousand years ago at the time of King Henry & Otto I — under the name of Magyars, another time under the name of Tartars, and still another time under the name of Genghis Khan and the Mongols.

Today they appear as Russians under the political banners of Bolshevism.

Heinrich Himmler

In late August 1944, as Soviet forces advance, & the actions of the Yugoslav partisans intensify, the Germans 'liquidate' the other lagers and the labor camp where Radnóti breathes each dying breath is abandoned. 3,600 prisoners are sent on a forced march back to Hungary.

At this time,
the poet begins his postcards from hell, the first being written in the
mountains on 30 August 1944 as the huge wild pulse of artillery from
Bulgaria beats on the mountain range making men, animals, wagons, and
thoughts swell, making even roads whinny and rear up like horses, mak-
ing even the sky gallop. An unknown *subjectum* endures within the poet
in this chaos, shining forever somewhere deep in his mind, without mov-
ing, silent, like the angel awed by death, or like an insect burying itself in
the rotted heart of a tree.

As the terrors continue, if not increase, *the word
still does not go silent in this poet;* it continues to persist, tenaciously,
sounding in him with every step, with each struggle, before all abjection,
with each hopeless day, a taut, finely-tuned thread. In the jaw of oblivion,
he writes, his recent sufferings recorded on 15 September 1944 in the
poem "Forced March," whose staccato rhythms, halted lines, and ten-
sionally spaced phrases evoke the strains, exactitude, & severities of the
march itself. To continue is a form of madness, but the body proceeds
as if adorned with wings, and although acquiescing in a ditch is a tempt-
ing relief, the strange hope that love and a sane and better death awaits
compel the prisoner on. But he knows, the poet knows, hope is a form of
madness, for nothing but the burned wind spins above and even walls lie
dead, plum trees are broken (it is the breaking of the Tree of Life), and
the angry night is thick with fear. He yearns to believe that everything
that is of value remains within, in his inner citadel, as does that most
foreign and unimaginable of things, a **(t)koimo-*, yet, if an exceedingly
tenuous hope, it is one, since many did return, just as the word continues
to persist in his body, a nearly omnipotent force, one as ever present as
death, if not coterminous with it:

This is how this poem walks up to you —
the words stamp quietly, then they fly up and crash,
just like death. And afterwards, a full, whishing
silence listens.

If the hope of his own survival is doubtful, before terror, before the sanguinary night, the poet's grasþ of the thread remains tenacious, stalwart — as the liquidations continue, on 17 September 1944, Radnóti makes copies of five of his poems and gives them to a friend, hoping he will emerge from the inferno, so as to bring the word to Radnóti's wife in safety, as his friend does. Missives from oblivion.

And in the notebook that will be discovered on his body after his death, he inscribes in five different languages a note stating that it contains the poetry of the Hungarian poet, Miklós Radnóti, who requests that the document be given to his friend Gyula Ortutay. That the notebook is complete with detailed printers' instructions also reinforces Radnóti's tenacious desire that the poems survive, that the word be received, that their form is considerably significant, & that, even in the midst of dying breaths, *he is thinking of each word scribed against oblivion not only as single words, but as a book, as a finished, printed work.*

Erőltetett menet
=   =

Bolond, ki földre rogyván   fölkél s újra lépdel,
s vándorló fájdalomként   mozdít bokát s térdet,
de mégis útnak indul,   mint akit szárny emel,
s hiába hívja árok,   maradni ~~úgyse~~ úgyse mer,
s ha kérdezed, miért nem?   ~~~~ még visszaszól talán,
hogy várja őt az asszony   s egy bölcsebb, szép halál.
Pedig bolond a jámbor,   mert ott az otthonok
fölött régóta már csak   a perzselt szél forog,
hanyattfekütt a házfal,   eltört a szilvafa,
s félelemtől bozhos   a honni éjszaka.
Ó, hogyha hinni tudnám: nemcsak szivemben hordom
mindazt, mit érdemes még,   s van visszatérni otthon;
ha volna még! s mint egykor   a régi hűs verandán
a béke méhe zöngne,   míg hűl a szilvalekvár,
s nyárvégi csönd napozna   az álmos kerteken,
a lomb közt gyümölcsök   ringnának meztelen,
s Fanni várna szőkén   a rőt sövény előtt,
s árnyékot írna lassan   a lassú délelőtt,
de hisz lehet talán még!   a hold ma oly kerek!
Ne menj tovább, barátom,   ~~~~ s fölkelek!
                              kiálts rám!

1944. szept. 15   Bor.

On this same day, the day of the copying of the poems, a column of 3,600 men is forced to march from Bor, moving under the heat of the sun, sleeping in fields at night. One man, who leaves the road to urinate, is shot dead. Another is killed for picking corn. Huddled together like beasts, the men subsist on scraps of bread, marmalade, spoonfuls of soup, raw carrots, squash. Still hungry, others enter the fields to pick corn — each is shot dead.

As the march continues, a German militia unit joins the guards and hundreds are executed on the road. The poet, his feet cracked with wounds, his mouth rife with abscesses, continues to write. Does he write in blood? Is his writing, even if in ink, a writing of blood? When they reach Ujvidék, for dinner, the men boil straw.

6 October 1944: while at Cservenka, Radnóti writes the second postcard from hell, noting that nine miles in the distance, haystacks and houses burn, most probably the result of the soldiers' destruction, all of which, as Radnóti observes, leaves the peasants in states of quiet fright.

7 October 1944: what is left of the column of men is divided into two groups, the first being taken to a large pit in a brickyard. The men are shot in blocks of 20 by SS troops. At dawn, the killing concludes. Momentarily.

The second group of men, of which Radnóti is part, encounters a troop of SS soldiers on horseback. Bored, the SS decide to make the men lie down in the road, then shoot at them at random. A death game. The violinist Miklós Lorsi, one of Radnóti's friends, is shot. He rises, struggling to continue marching. Radnóti and another man come to his aid. Sarcastic, an SS man shouts: *Der springt noch auch!* then shoots Lorsi again, killing him, his body rolling over the poet, making his own death ever more palpable, ever more concrete, ever more inevitable. It is as if this death is a preparation for his, nearly buried alive as he is with his friend.

14 October 1944: the column of men reach a tanning yard in Mohács, where they remain for weeks and unload towboats. As Radnóti writes ten days later in his third postcard from hell, the oxen drool blood, the men urinate it, and the squad is like a tangled knot, stinking and mad while death, some hideous Bosch-like beast, seethes overhead, a terrible, pestiferous wind.

The column travels by boxcar to Szentkirályszabadja. On 31 October 1944, nearly three weeks after witnessing his friend's murder, Radnóti writes the final postcard from hell, inscribing it on the back of a medicine bottle label. With whatever means necessary, the word must be recorded:

> I fell next to him. His body rolled over.
> It was tight as a string before it snaps.
> Shot in the back of the head — "This is how
> you'll end." "Just lie quietly," I said to myself.
> Patience flowers into death now.
> "*Der springt noch auf,*" I heard above me.
> Dark filthy blood was drying on my ear.

Radnóti is compelled to describe what he witnesses, to record, with the most tenuous of hopes, or with courageous fragility, brutalities and barbarities — will they be heard? will they survive the silence? will they survive the hunger of worms? —, writing in the midst of disaster, *writing the disaster itself*, giving us a poetic record of an Inferno. Poetry is his anchor, & his poem to his friend Lorsi, is his last…

It is to poetry that Radnóti calls, not to a god; it is a daring Marsyas that he becomes, risking his flesh doubly before a merciless *&* savage Apollo, for he will not cast his aulos to the turf of the riverbank, even in the face of terror, no, he will court disaster threefold.

In early November, during a day march, the guards continue their death games, this time making the men run. Those who collapse are shot.

At Pannonhalma, on 6 November 1944, Radnóti is beaten, his face and head scarred with gashes. Is his notebook discovered? Do they learn of his allegiance to the word? Or do they just beat him for fun?

On 8 November 1944, 22 of the men, some of the last of the original column of 3,600, wounded *&* gravely ill, are tossed onto ox-carts like battered meat and taken to a hospital in Győr. They are turned away due to overcrowding, or refused.

Hungarian soldiers, accompanied by two Austrian SS, order the forced laborers to march toward the Western borders of Hungary.

They don't need privacy, to kill in secret, since they can murder indiscriminately, under the open sky. As the Nazis frequently said to their victims, *Tomorrow you'll be wiggling skyward as smoke from this chimney…* Murder is only entertainment. They force the men to march out of boredom, just to have something to do. How many different ways can they kill?

When they reach a field near a dam on the Rábca River, the guards borrow a hoe from a local inn, tools from the dam keeper's wife, then order the laborers to dig a ditch.

Too weak to complete the task, the guards dig the hole instead, then order several prisoners to jump in the ditch to smooth it out.

One by one, the men are shot. The insect sound rips through the air. Miklós Radnóti is dead, as are his stepmother and sister, both of whom are murdered in Auschwitz. The fields preserve his bones.

The final prisoner is ordered to cover the bodies with dirt. Once finished, he is beaten to death with the tools, which are then returned to their respectful owners.

On 23 June 1946, the mass grave in Abda is discovered and the exhumed bodies are taken to Győr to be buried in the local Jewish cemetery on 25 June 1946. Autopsies are performed. The official death of Corpse # 12, Miklós Radnóti, is listed as death by gunshot to the skull.

He is identified through documents found in his clothes which include his name card, his civil identity card, his membership to the Economic Association of Writers, an authorized copy of his baptism certificate, letters addressed in his name, and a small black notebook containing his poems. Radnóti is buried for the second time. The price of immortality — dying again & again & again.

On 16 August 1946, over a month and a half later, Radnóti is removed from the cemetery in Győr & buried for the third & final time in Fiumei úti nemzeti sírkert, Budapest.

In each surviving word, does his breath not exist?

Offenbarung Der Judischen Rassenseele!

And so, during a revolt in 477 A D, the Imperial Library of Constan-
tinople is incinerated, 120,000 volumes burning, like flesh to ash, a copy
of the *Iliad* on a twelve-foot snakeskin turning, twisting in the flames,
water bled from skin like tears.

Beware the Book?

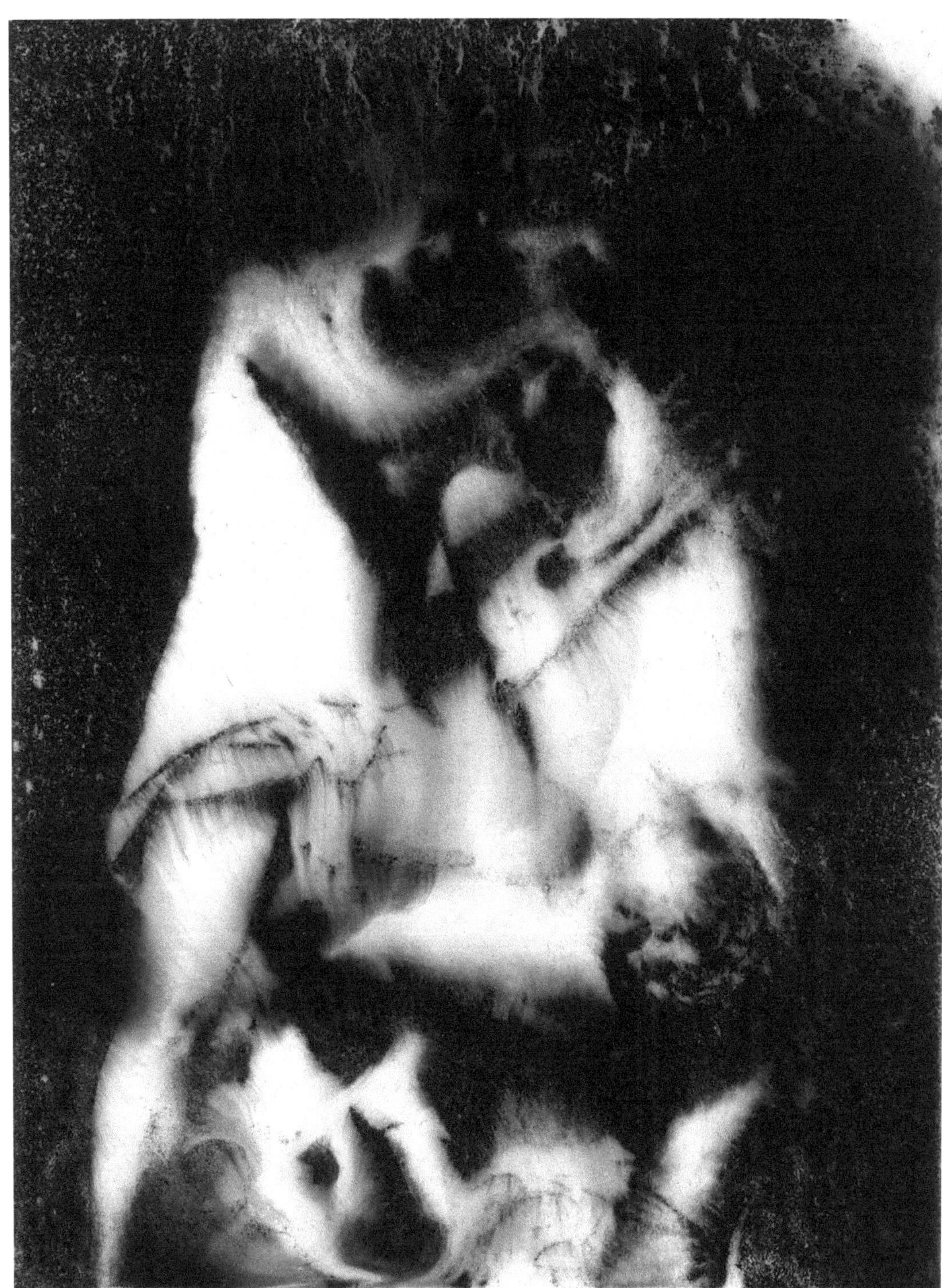

To sustain the   t-e---------n------------s------------------i-o---n
                of one THREAD
                is to enact a   necessary violence
a-
gain-st

                        the other.
                Here is our anguish;
                here is our movement

  in-
to
a
nar-
row:
                our suffering
                        under
                two dynamic forces
                like a planet
                        tilting
                      & spinning
                        under
                the force
                of
gra-
v

i

ty

        .

PROHIBITION!

"Narrated Ibn Abbas: When the Prophet saw pictures in the Ka'ba, he did not enter it till he ordered them to be erased. ... 'May Allah curse them!'" — Sahih Bukhari

"A'isha reported that Allah's Messenger entered and I had hung a thin curtain having pictures on it. The color of his face underwent a change. He then took hold of that curtain and tore it and then said: The most grievous torment for the people on the Day of Resurrection would be for those who try to imitate Allah in the act of creation." — Sahih Muslim

"I am going to narrate to you what I heard from Allah's Messenger. I heard him say: All the painters who make pictures would be in the fire of Hell. The soul will be breathed in every picture prepared by him and it shall punish him in Hell, and he said: If you have to do it at all, then paint the pictures of trees & lifeless things; and Nasr b. 'Ali confirmed it." — Sahih Muslim

Carte
Ethnographique
d'Europe

One of the premises and incentives for my poetry is disgust.

What I revolted against was that it had survived the end of the world
as though nothing had happened.

The production of 'beauty' to induce 'esthetic experiences' strikes me
as a harmless but ludicrous and childish preoccupation.

Różewicz

καλλον
επηλεξον
καλαπτανεκ
τετρους
ωτς
υστεφανιτρον
ερμηνεας
εαδελεσ
[illegible]
[illegible]
πεντηκοντε
ηπεωσ
[illegible]φιλοντ[illegible]
[illegible]τρισ[illegible]
[illegible]
[illegible]περιτων
κνω[illegible]
[illegible]φανιρον
αντρον[illegible]

When he decides to move to Paris, he cannot foresee the consequences that will arise, or that his departure from Berlin will be the onset of a new, even longer, and equally if not perhaps greater period of anguished wandering and dislocation, the even ſtranger and more extreme suſpension of his life, of living in a far more radical ſtate of *entre-temps*, of *entre-eſpace*, of *entre-pays*, and that the rupture, the fraƈture, the shattering, is increasing within him; — the thread is being ſtretched more and more taut as the ſtate of *Unheimlichness* is pitched to an ever higher degree, for the expanse between him and his library is increasing, ſplitting in various direƈtions, with oceans and borders between them, bi- and tri-furcating him across ſpace-time, for his turn to Paris will firſt be brief, and he will be forced to leave books there as well before departing to the mountains of Umbria for one month, where he will exiſt as if nowhere, in relative silence, at laſt recovering his solitude, though only briefly. It will upon refleƈtion seem like a ſtrange dream, as if he had never perhaps even gone there, as if it was an imagined journey, with only his memory (and the memory of whom he encountered — did they encounter him?) as proof, for his passſport had not been ſtamped. It was an idyllic period, a time of peace and tranquility, of personal harmony. There was a ſtrange correlation between him and the village too because it was so high up in the mountains that it was often if not generally enveloped by a cloud. Little did he realize that it would not be for another year that he would at laſt be truly alone, and it would not be for nearly another year that he would finally have a room of his own.

From the mountains of Umbria he turns back to Paris, but only for two months. It is a time of both intense physical ecſtasy, of a certain kind of intoxicated erotic bliss, and a sharp, searing mental anguish, for he is possessed by the exaƈting burden of an immense editing task, philological work never before enaƈted in hiſtory, and he carries the pressure of this burden in his every nerve, every minute of every day, *&* it is work that demands the moſt acute attention, twelve to more hours a day, all week, without reſt, provoking ſtates of extreme emotional volatility, which result in outwardly direƈted explosions. All those who do not wish to align themselves with these tasks, which he sees as worldly ones with a great historical aim, all those who lend no alliance to the pursuit, before them he is silent, removed. In fact, he sees them as traitors to culture & civilization, especially those whose devotion to this heritage is broken through procreating, a criminal act at this world juncture.

*   *   *   *   *

Since he does not want the bliss to cease, he must depart Paris and, yet again, he must bury his belongings in a cave, though with the intention of soon returning, to at last make *les racines*, to at last reach his true destination, to at last construct a sanctuary, to at last *cease moving*. What he longs for is to draw as tight a circumference around himself as possible, to live as if in a tower, to press downward into the earth, not outward into space, across the sea, or across the sky, but to be still, to not venture beyond even the Périphérique.

The ceaseless movement separates him further & further from having a protective & necessary solitude, without which he cannot write. He is further & further from having an abode in which to isolate himself, further & further from the word, from reading, from writing, further & further from a necessary silence, closer & closer *à un état inquiétant* — despite the fact that several books have been forming in him for some time, it has now been several years since he has completed a new one. Because he must edit all day long, once he finishes, he is too enervated to even think of reading or writing, and so the book that he has envisioned writing, the book that hovers at the far edge of his thoughts, *Toward a Genealogy of the Sublime*, remains suspended. He actually no longer reads, but only *edit-reads*, a strange type of repetitive and monotonous non-reading that eventually makes him despise books. He refers to himself no longer as a person but as an *editorial homunculus*. It is this work that makes him *ex-centric*, which keeps him from his citadel; in this, he submits himself to a dangerous experiment, a digression & dispersion that may ruin him. He has come to a disturbingly paradoxical position — *the word keeps him from the word.*

He cannot foresee the consequences that will arise in New York, or that his return across the Atlantic will result in his thread growing ever more taut, ever more tense, ever thinner, ever more fragile, though he does this time have a sense of foreboding and fears that the journey will be exacting. He does not want to go. The city is dead to him, as the country, and he has no desire to ever return, save to recover his library, but due to the precariousness of his life, to its utter instability, the recovery of his library is as improbable an event as is walking from Persia to the Orion Nebula. As his ancestors left long ago, he wants to reverse the malady of their migration, of a centuries old dislocation that gnaws at him at the molecular level; to recover something autochthonous. Even though he realizes such a recovery is improbable, conceptually, the idea of reverse migration acts as a utopic force, a critical force, a power that combats excessive rationalism, which courts the impossible, which seeks the thing against which it can shatter.

*   *   *   *   *

Drive your cart & your plow
over the bones of the dead

And so, when asked what to do with the books of the Library of Alexandria, Caliph Umar says,

If the content of the books is in accordance with the Book of Allah, we may do without them, for in that case, the Book of Allah more than suffices. If, on the other hand, they contain no matter not in accordance with the Book of Allah, there can be no need to preserve them. Proceed, then, and destroy them.

And so, the minions of the Caliph distribute the books of Alexandria to the public baths, to feed the stoves that warm the publicum.

And there were so many books that it took six months to incinerate the mass of thought.

No books but steam; no books but clean bodies — forget science, forget learning, only pray in obeisance. But is not to pray *to prey on* consciousness?

Beware the Book?

Beware the Caliph.

As the one-armed poet rests his stump on his desk, engulfed by silence, his personality eclipsed, Beckett places grenades next to geraniums like spacing out words on a page, and Radnóti inscribes word after measured word against silence, against terror, the precision of his form struggling against the monstrosity of a particular & exacting chaos, René Char is in Céreste, between 52 & 77 km from Aix-en-Provence, 35 km from Roussillon, & over 1400–1500 kilometers from the places where, moment to moment, Radnóti knowingly confronts death.

After having fought with the 173rd regiment of heavy artillery in the Battle of Alsace, former Surrealist René Char is demobilized in 1940. He returns home to L'Isle-sur-la-Sorgue only to be swiftly denounced by Jean Poutet, President of the Legion, for Gaullist activity. Surveillance begins. Mail is observed. Char is endangered, as is his wife, Georgette Goldstein, who Poutet also denounces.

The Germans approach. The poet's arrest is imminent. The long period of homelessness begins. He flees his birthplace, crisscrossing the region like a crab, moving east, moving north, under cover of the leaves, of trees, of shadows, till he reaches the Basses Alpes & holes up in Céreste where, as Capitaine Alexandre, he establishes links with other members of the Resistance in Céreste, Digne, and the surrounding areas. Are Cendrars & Beckett, both of whom are on the "Otto List," amongst this circle? What validity does the word have for Capitaine Alexandre? How does its pressure bear against him, with what force, with what urgency, with what resolve? How does being manifest itself in him? How receptive is he to the sounding of such an ontological power?

As Radnóti writes his Second Eclogue, Capitaine Alexandre is engaging in armed opposition as part of the *Armée Secrète*, in charge of the section Durance-Sud, but the effects of this resistance do not reach Radnóti. And while the Hungarian poet endures his second and longest period of forced labor, Capitaine Alexandre is commandeering partisan groups of the *Forces Françaises Combattantes* in the Alpes de Provence, but this does not seem to affect Radnóti, who is writing of the shattering of reality, of the poet who continues to teach in measure and form but, because all things fall apart, can only sit and gaze, because, as he says, *nothing can be done*. Does Capitaine Alexandre think of Lorca's assassination, too, if it is a prelude to his own death? Is not the death of one poet the death of all poets?

*

7 September 1943
Himmler to the Higher SS & Police Chief
Ukraine, Kiev

The aim to be achieved is that when areas in the Ukraine are evacuated, not a human being, not a single head of cattle, not a bag of grain, not a railroad track remains behind; not a house remains standing, not a mine exists which is not ruined for years to come, not a well which is not poisoned. The enemy must really find a totally scorched & destroyed country... Do everything that is humanly possible.

*

Chief of seven regions of the Maquis, Capitaine Alexandre oversees parachute landings of arms and munitions. Under the Hitlerian Night, although the word does not go silent in Char, although the word proliferates in him, Capitaine Alexandre refuses to publish, even in clandestine journals, and so for six years, if not impeded by it, his word is suffused with silence. Under the monstrous Arc of Saturn, there can be no sense of normalcy, but the terrors, the horrors, the acts of devastation, the fears — all events must be recorded, for the poet is a prism who transfigures reality thru his veins & nerves after, like some Rimbaudian *voyant*, he encounters the cataclysms of reality, confronts poisons, torments, positions himself at a threshold of extreme risk, whereby he may perish, *but he courts every possible form of decimation out of a willingness to acquire knowledge.* Out of terrible readiness. What is vital here is not victory, but reaching that which is unknown, and in this we glimpse one of the Gospels of Failure, where it is the *test*, the *experiment*, the *leap* that is of import — not the outcome of such ventures. *Expenditure.* Pressing against impossibility, the vortex of disaster is brought under the poet's instruments: the microscope, the telescope, the X-ray. There is no belief in representation. It is clear. The principle is long dead. What is realism to a surrealist, or to any poet worth his salt? One of the poet's instruments is also the kaleidoscope. What is given to language, what logos itself demands be inscribed, are horrors, cruelties, abominations; desecrations of the most vile kind. Is it that no poetry after — or, to be even more exacting, *during* — Auschwitz is possible, or that we can not bear the demand of the word, the image, the tone, the scent (is there an artist of scents? a tragic *scentist?*) that rises within us with such energy that it forces us to record even its shards, its febrile reverberations, its distant and pale echoes, its short-circuits, its schismatic irruptions as they rise in our veins? Still, in the midst of impending disaster, of actual disaster, some write, some record, some *kaleidoscope* reality; still, before our knowledge of erasure, of desecration, of knowledge become fragmentary (the burnt tablets of Ashurbanipal, the ashen remainders of the Sybilline Books, the shards of Sappho, Menander, & Sophocles, the desiccated relics of the Persian Royal Archives, the scorched Mayan codices) or legend, some continue, knowing oblivion is before us, knowing the entire earth may one day be reconstituted, or obliterated, become nothing but a dead rock that reflects light, like the moon and other unknown moons, former life-bearing planets, in millenniums before ours — how can we know? Dark matter obstructs the search for knowledge; time breaks us against its immeasurable distances. *What will happen to our artifacts?* Will they become fossilized? Or nothing but indecipherable refuse; the debris of space, the Voynich pulp of the future? Before this knowledge, Char writes what will become the *Leaves of Hypnos*, & he writes knowingly of the ephemerality of his gesture:

Ces notes n'empruntent rien à l'amour de soi, à la nouvelle, à la maxime
ou au roman. Un feu d'herbes sèches eut tout aussi bien été leur éditeur.

  The title contains this knowledge too, a work as fragile & impermanent as a leaf, which lasts but a season then bursts into flame-like colors, then falls, then crumbles and disintegrates, crushed under foot, or incinerated, like a pyre, or burnt offering… The leaf too, the leaf of the page, the carrier of the word, the leaves of Hypnos the leaves of a sleeping and forgotten god, leaves which can also burst into flame. And the ephemerality of the work, its insignificance, is made evident in atrocity. For the thread can be broken by barbarism; silence can usurp the word, or our ability to listen, when we are reduced to the human, all too human and lose the *sub specie æternitatis* perspective:

    La vue du sang supplicié en a fait une fois perdre le fil,
     à réduit a néant leur importance.
Elles furent écrites dans la tension, la colère, la peur, l'émulation,
le dégoût, la ruse, le recueillement furtif,
    l'illusion de l'avenir, l'amitié, l'amour,
C'est dire combine elles sont affectées par   *l'événement…*

  The cataclysms, the torments, the poisons, the possible and actual decimations, they are encountered in executions, in tortures, in murders, in the capturing & deportation of friends & comrades, just as hope, however tenuous, is encountered in the parachuting of arms & of men.

  In the search for knowledge, Rimbaud spoke of undergoing unspeakable torments, that confronting such requires *complete faith and superhuman strength* (he was not speaking of the middling poets that would come after him, of those for whom poetry is a game, a pastime, *poesy*), for they are powerful enough to reduce one to an invalid, to make one into a master criminal. Is not the bearer of such knowledge in some way contaminated, someone who has come into contact with toxins, like Pandora opening the pithos? All knowledge is not positive; it is also terrible, abominable, threatening, as the ancient Greeks knew, the Delphic Oracle commanding not only *gnothi seauton* but also *meden agan,* which Pindar echoes with his epigram: *Keep the measure of wisdom.* But there are events which press upon *&* against one's will, which bear down on us like gravity, such as the horrific day Capitaine Alexandre speaks of, when immobilized before the execution of a friend:

            Gun in hand, he and others of the resistance are situated on the heights overlooking Céreste, armed so heavily the bushes creak, armed as sufficiently as the SS, who are not aware of their presence.

            Pivoting about, alert as falcons, armed to advantage, all at Capitaine Alexandre's command await his signal. They are ready to open fire. Mais, il répond, *non* — une terrible, angoisse, torturés . . . . . <u>NON</u>.

At that instant, June he says slipped a polar chill into his bones: they
watch B. fall, light as a leaf, light enough that even "the least breath of
wind could have lifted him from the earth." The body as ephemeral as a
wisp of smoke. If he gave the signal and all of the SS were assassinated,
the Nazis would have returned and decimated the entire village. "What
is a village?" Did B., Capitaine Alexandre asks at the end of one of these
leaves of Hypnos, perhaps know that he had to be sacrificed to save the
village? Did he see Capitaine Alexandre? Did he sense him from afar?
Another terrible form of knowledge, though perhaps one that enables B.
to endure the bullets with stalwart equanimity as they sear toward him,
ready to char his flesh, to carbonize him.

The precariousness of existence,
its tenuousness, is evident in the form of the *Feuillets d'Hypnos*, with its
fragmentary, isolated texts, each a missive from oblivion, each perhaps the
last word, none truly tethered to any other, for order, logic, regularity —
such do not exist at this moment, even if the planet spins as it has always
spun. It is a time of explosiveness. Of human and ontological schisms.
Of strife, agon, and death; of the shattering force of being itself, render-
ing us as it suffuses us, giving and taking breath, giving and taking blood,
giving and taking flesh, sculpting and destroying, sculpting by destroying,
and plainly destroying. The word does not die in Char but reflects the
exacting pulse of his epoch: threat, risk, tragedy, pessimism, hypocrisy,
each moment, even each second, sometimes pregnant with the violent
sculpting force of being. This is a period whose every moment is rife with
potentiality, when each *kairos* is truly decisive. And before the monstros-
ity irrupting in history, *the poet centers himself in the storm, desubjectivizes
himself* to assure the coming again of justice:

*Certaines époques de la condition de
l'homme subissent l'assaut glacé d'un
mal qui prend appui sur les points les
plus déshonorés de la nature humaine.*

But then, even our cataclysms, even the atrocities we have endured, witnessed, & meticulously documented, however strong the force of our ethics, *none of them will remain.* The species will perish, the planet will perish; both will become nothing but specks of dust drifting through the cosmos, just as the specks of dust now drifting about us are perchance the indecipherable remnants of other immeasurably distant, earlier eons, the ashes of … a *prelude*, the ashes of those who have been burned.

As Char notes in one leaf, the soul is mortal, but before a disjointed epoch, where all forms are shattered, the word still lives & rises out of us, persisting like geysers from the depths of the earth. Poetry says Char is "*la part imaginaire qui, elle aussi, est susceptible d'action,*" for words are "a form of action, the concretized perpetuity of this fugitive Action." Poetry is here *a living force,* just as it is for Radnóti, inscribing in the dark, marking pages before oblivion. Yet, this living force may equally be obliterated, just as Radnóti's poems may never have been discovered, Char's *Leaves of Hypnos* may have found its end in a blaze of fire, or been devoured by the earth itself as it lay hidden in a hole of a wall in Céreste.

For writing is both a form of firefight and that which may be consumed by fire, forever destroyed, a single work, perhaps of little significance, lost forever (there was no guarantee that, upon returning from Algiers, he would find the leaves), or worse, the record of a civilization forever destroyed in an instant, the terror which rose in Nietzsche upon learning of the fires and the destruction in Paris in 1871, and the terror which arose in the Jews of Paris in 1244 when 24 carriage loads of Talmuds & other Jewish religious manuscripts were set on fire in the streets of Paris.

c'etait mais un prelude

Nearly 700 years later, an arms drop before daybreak. Capitaine Alexandre's ironic code word for this action is *la bibliothèque est en feu.* The parachute descending, the crate striking the ground, the crate detonating on impact: — the surrounding forest bursts into flame. Could it have been an arms drop that saved Radnóti? Is it always certain that out of such infernos culture, civilization, the muses, can be regenerated? Have the Aztecs *&* the Mayans recovered from the Conquistadors? How many civilizations have been derailed by conquering forces? And what have we in place of them, in place of the vigor of such cultures? Or will a silence such as no other silence come to reign? The noisy silence of capitalism? Will it eradicate the forces that gave birth to such manifestations? An ineradicable trauma that renders all things mute? A trauma that breaks the scales of existence? Who ever anywhere will read these written words? Signs on a white field. The word is a form of hope against trauma, or a record that carries trauma within it, *embodies* wounds, if it can withstand the shattering force, a force which itself seeks to be recorded and is in constant war with poiesis.

Bolshevistic!

And so, when Hisham and the Berber Generals seize control of the Caliphate of Cordoba, Berber tribes sack the city, destroying its palaces, slaughtering thousands, destroying almost all of the volumes of the Library of Al-Hakkam II.

Beware the Book?

Beware the Extinguishers of Knowledge.

The MANIFESTATION
                    of the THREAD
                        is s~u~f~fuse~d
              with extreme danger,
                        the FRISSON
                        of EXISTENCE,
                    the shivering ecstasy
                        of LIFE
                                IN THIS,
                                the CATA-STROPHIC
                                should be HEARD,
                            for this MANIFESTATION
                                is an   EXILE
into the   *Unheimlich*
where the other

drags
a-
gain-st
it
with unsettling force,
like
the
un
der
tow
of
the
sea,
re
a
sser
ting
its
fundamental dominion
        over our gnosis
        over our will to power

that which in-vol-ves
the   constant,
                necessary,
inexorable threat

of DIS-ASTER

SHATTERING

is *intrinsic*
to
ex-
is-
tence
it-self.

EROS *&* STRIFE

cell suicide

en-

tro-

p
y
.

We are dealing with a nation of high culture, with "a people of the
Book"... The Germans have simply gone crazy for one thing — books ...
Where plunder is based on an ideology, on a world outlook which in
essence is ſpiritual, it cannot be equaled in ſtrength and durability...
The Nazi has both book and sword, and this is his ſtrength and might.

Chaim Aron Kaplan

Drive your cart & your plow over the bones of the dead!

The Mefiste Haskalah Library

In the Ghetto of Vilna, in the midst of monstrous acts & bestial events, with the threat of deportation always at hand, the Jews build a library, scavenged from private collections and synagogues. To Herman Kruk, the librarian overseeing the desiccated collection, the arrival of each new Torah scroll is a brutish addition, for they signify the destruction of one more Jewish community — each Torah is equivalent to a gravestone. Kruk therefore shrouds them in sheets & conceals them in the archives.

Although many of the books have dozens of missing pages, often non-existent margins due to frequent rebinding, with lines vanishing in the vortex of each book's spine, it is immaterial: even if fragmented, broken, or disfigured, readers devour them. The material aspect of each book echoing each reader's hunger. Eventually, Kruk reports, the library will be left with empty shelves, each absent book the equivalent of each absent prisoner of war, each human leaf. Yet, and it is an exacting contrast, in the midst of atrocities and horrors, before ever increasing savageness, 100,000 books circulate, all of which Kruk carefully documents, noting that, of the books borrowed, 78.3% are literature, 17.7% are children's literature, and 4% are non-fiction. Reading, *hunger for the word*, even if it is to escape, or to look the devil in the face, *continues*. It is a bulwark, a void, a drug. *Léthē*. A critical force. *A weapon*. Before the prelude, *to read* is to commit a transgression. To oppose.

July 1943

Liquidation of the Ghetto Begins

20,000 books are chosen
to be shipped to Germany.
What remains is pulped —
transporting & storing them
will incur expenses.
To create room for an illegal shipment of hogs,
Dr. Pohl
tosses five cases of   rare books
off the train.

And so, Eustathius, Archbishop of Thessaloniki, says,

You treat this as a matter of trade, selling off this advantage you possess, indeed listening to the suggestions of the evil spirit who tells you, "Sell these Books of yours, spend the money as you please and follow me"…
You illiterate fool, why ever do you wish to reduce the library to the level of your own character? Just because you have no trace of culture, must you empty the library of the books that transmit it?

Beware the Book?
Beware the Illiterate Fool.
Beware the Philistine.

In September 1943, Herman Kruk is deported to Estonia.

In September 1944, in the Kruga Concentration Camp,
                    he   wiggles   skyward ~

PROHIBITION!

"Neither in content nor in form is art the highest and absolute mode of bringing to our minds the true interests of the spirit. For precisely on account of its form, art is limited to a specific content. Only one sphere and stage of truth is capable of being represented in the element of art. In order to be a genuine content for art, such truth must in virtue of its own specific character be able to go forth into sense and remain adequate to itself there. This is the case, for example, with the gods of Greece. On the other hand, there is a deeper comprehension of truth which is no longer so akin and friendly to sense as to be capable of appropriate adoption and expression in this medium. The Christian view of truth is of this kind, and, above all, the spirit of our world today, or, more particularly, of our religion and the development of our reason, appears as beyond the stage at which art is the supreme mode of our knowledge of the Absolute. The peculiar nature of artistic production and or works of art no longer fills our highest need."

Hegel

On peut brûler la bibliothèque d'Alexandrie.
Au-dessus et en dehors des papyrus, il y a des forces:

> *on nous enlèvera pour quelque temps la faculté*
de retrouver ces forces,

on ne supprimera pas leur énergie.

> *Et il est bon que de trop grandes facilités*
disparaissent

> *et que des formes tombent*
> *en oubli*

et la culture sans espace ni temps,
et que détient notre capacité nerveuse
reparaîtra avec une énergie accrue.

Et il juste que de temps en temps

> *des cataclysmes se produisent*
qui nous incitent
à en revenir à la nature.
c'est-à-dire à retrouver la vie.

Antonin Artaud

No People
lives
longer
than the documents of its
culture.

— Hitler

And so, under the reign of Muhammed Bakhtiyar Khilji, Muslim invaders sack and destroy Odantapuri University and its Library, with fires so voluminous they burn for months.

The decline of Buddhism in India is provoked.
All hail fire!
No more buddhas, no more books — weapons, a fortress!
Beware the Book?
Beware Marauding Invaders.
Beware the Bibliophobes.

Upon returning to NYC, out of desperation and necessity, Renato takes on the position of caretaker to Jakob, a former psychoanalyst from Vienna (he fled Europe during the reign of the Nazis) who, due to his wife having died some months ago, is extremely despondent. Renato cooks for him, provides companionship, and manages his offices and daily affairs. But Jakob is more than despondent; he is death-obsessed. Nonetheless, Renato manages to frequently make him laugh. When he tells Jakob he is a strict Marxist & the old man asks, "Are you a western-, libertarian-, or neo-Marxist?" Renato replies, "A Harpo Marxist…," a joke the doctor frequently remembers and laughs at anew.

Despite his sometimes-cheerful moments, Jakob's temper is morbid. Although his body is decrepit, most of his teeth missing, and his health poor, permitting him only to shuffle around with a walker, he believes he will be able to fly to Switzerland for an assisted suicide. The degree to which his family takes seriously this desire, and the impact of it on those around him, is questionable. What he requires is not a caretaker, but a nurse. Every day, Jakob asks if his new passport has arrived.

For many weeks, Renato tends to him, cooks for him, and manages his affairs. Due to the high degree of Renato's porousness, Jakob's distemper seeps into him, affects him at the cellular level, and he is pained by Jakob's misery. Throughout this time, Renato continues the philological task he began in Paris, still burdened by the exacting duty of it, a work he seeks to make perfect. Guided by this ethic, his nights are anxious, tense, sleepless; ruled by the word, ruled by his homunculus existence, an extreme form of self-erasure. In some way, just as his books are delimited, inert, reposing tomes, he too is equally non-existent: a perpetually hovering creature, limen, or geo-tertium quid. A barbarophonoist. And just as a cloud, he could dissipate; vanish as if he had never even existed, or be nothing more than a sprite, some form of cold plasma. There is though some small comfort in being in Jakob's townhouse, for its walls are lined from floor to ceiling with books, and Renato drifts *&* floats *&* wanders amongst them, peruses them as he once did his own, so they can suffuse him, speak to him from afar, call to him, and he feels that, eventually, perhaps he will at last recover his own library, perhaps he will no longer be a homunculus, nor a cloud or a jellyfish, but a reader, someone *avec les racines*, someone who roams through long periods of time, knowing he is not excluded from any age, but has access to them all, knowing he can annex every age to his own, knowing that he can have concourse with the vast lineage of the past.

Over time, Jakob grows more *&* more attached to Renato, calls for him to be by his side continuously, making it increasingly difficult for him to have any moments of peace or solitude. Because Renato is staying in Jakob's townhouse, in some way Jakob feels like he owns him, as if he is not an employee, but a servant upon whom he can call at any moment he wishes, that Renato no longer has a will of his own, but is a kind of animal that can be harnessed, if not discarded, for servants, like domestic pets, are dispensable. Although the servant is present during the holiday, it is never part of the holiday. The servant is a disembodied figure. A phantom.

Instead of eating but a few times a day, Jakob requests that Renato cook for him nearly every three hours, making him feel more and more possessed, more and more invaded, more and more enslaved. Is this increasing hunger, as the need to possess, not a form of radical inner vacuity? Whenever Jakob senses that Renato is in the midst of a thought, that he is growing independent, as if fearing an independence that forever distances him, Jakob calls to him, *&* if he does not appear in his room immediately, Jakob shouts his name again and again, his voice desperate, demanding, possessive. He knows that, although Renato is attentive, perhaps dutiful, he remains isolated, his will beyond anyone's grasp, something within him impenetrable, separate from the world. Solitary. Although typically calm, a state which makes many people believe they can dominate him, Renato does not ever succumb to anyone's will and frequently, if not generally, rarely expresses his true thoughts for, like an alchemist, he speaks with unreserved freedom only to others he knows have reached similar pinnacles of thought, others who are as emancipated and amoral. Externally, he has the *Schein* of someone normal, but his eyes betray him as someone who wants to tear most of the world into pieces and completely transform it, to dismantle edifices and institutions and build anew, from dust to star.

One morning, Jakob shuffles out of his room in a highly distressed state. He tells Renato that he has been up all night long researching how to commit suicide. Drawing his hand across his throat, he says, "I cannot do it this way because it is too painful," recounts other ways that are also too grim or complicated for him, then says: "I'm going to give you $500 and you are going to go out & buy me a handgun so I can shoot myself in the head."

Despite believing in free death, Renato doesn't think that this is the ideal way to enact it, and he is disturbed by Jakob's request, explaining that he will be implicated, that those who would adjudicate the event would view him as an accomplice to a crime. But Jakob insists, tells Renato that he can just wear gloves and buy a gun on the street. Growing ever more scurrilous, Jakob curses the fact that he ever let his children take his gun away from him because he wants to pierce his skull *now, this instant,* yearns for that scintillating moment of intolerable but ecstatic pain, of his head being coactired. *The anguish must end.* What is particularly unsettling for Renato is the fact that, just last night, he discovered the gun by chance. Due to his memory not being entirely perfect, Jakob has forgotten that it remains in his possession; that it is within arm's reach of his bed, ready-to-hand.

Eventually, Renato helps Jakob to reach a state of relative calm and, once he is asleep, Renato calls Jakob's son to inform him of the incident, but his son says that he will not be able to make it to the house for several days, a period of great tension and stress, for Renato could not recover the gun. He waits second after second, hour after hour, day after day, night after night, waits for a loud bang to ring out, or to be accidentally shot himself.

In the ensuing days, Jakob, who said that only wine eases his pain, drinks more and more frequently, his mien getting stranger and stranger, as if he is undergoing a metamorphosis, some subtle but definite & irreversible form of mutation that no one can circumvent. One day, he takes a siesta after drinking an entire bottle of wine, his lips purple, his eyes noir. Renato notices that Jakob's personality seems different, an effect due not just to the wine, but to something more extreme, to an inner schism, to some possible disintegration of the psyche.

After returning from lunch, Renato is working in the living room, in the midst of at last finalizing his great philological task, when a loud bang echoes through the townhouse. Running into Jakob's room, he finds him on the ground, naked, a light smashed, his bathrobe and pajamas twisted around his ankles, him howling repeatedly, making dreadful screeching noises, shouting at Renato, elongating each syllable: *"Re-na-to, I pissed my-self, I shit my-self… Re-na-to…"*

As he glances around the room, Renato sees that it is soiled with shit, that Jakob has smeared his feces on the floor and walls, knocked over his plants, torn objects to pieces, and that his eye is swollen & purple and there is a gash on his forehead that is caked and dry.

As Renato returns from the bathroom with hot towels to clean Jakob, the room goes deafeningly silent — the *écrasement* has come. The sound of a gunshot silences the howling. A body slumps to the floor. The scent of gunpowder mingles with the putrid one of feces and urine, a minuscule

cloud of smoke dissipating in the room, Jakob's body inert, his fragile
skull cracked open, his head split in pieces, the blood brains and shattered
bits of cranium diffused in multiple directions.

Renato turns, slowly walks into the other room, sits before the wild ar-
ray of plants that stretch nearly to the ceiling, then wraps the hot towels
around his neck.

He gazes up at the skylight in silence, watching as the snow falls, as
the light of the moon pierces the glass, making the leaves of the plants
shimmer.

*   *   *   *   *

The tradition of the oppressed teaches us that the 'state of emergency' in which we live is not the exception but the rule. We must attain to a conception of history that is in keeping with this insight. Then we shall clearly realize that it is our task to bring about a real state of emergency, and this will improve our position in the struggle against Fascism. One reason why Fascism has a chance is that in the name of progress its opponents treat it as a historical norm. The current amazement that the things we are experiencing are 'still' possible in the 20th century is not philosophical. This amazement is not the beginning of knowledge — unless it is the knowledge that the view of history which gives rise to it is untenable.

Walter Benjamin
Theses on the Philosophy of History
1940

The *Unzeitgemäße,*
       those broken,
      malformed creatures,
   each who twiſt,
       turn their bodies
againſt time
   againſt broken time

             TO P~E~E~R
             through all of
             HISTORY

        & into caves
      so as to give birth to u~~n~~~i~~t~~e~~d
T---------------------I--------------------M--------------------E
       those who see darkness & light
             intertwined
     for they resiſt the blitzkrieg
    of empty ſpectacles

        those who see
THE
S------------H-----------A-----------D-----------O-----------W

     those who marry darkness
  a force that continuously approaches them
as if by magnetic power

   the ebb & flow of shadow & light
      like waves,
    a fierce ontological current
   which approaches & recedes
      which appears & withdraws
    which withholds…

And so, following the Disputation of Paris, 10 to 12,000 Talmuds &
other Jewish religious manuscripts are set on fire in the streets of Paris.

Heresy, obscenity, error, imbecility.

All Hail Nicholas Donin!

Joshua must become Geronimo, Solomon must become Paul, and
Jesus will not be condemned to boiling excrement!

Beware the Book?

Beware the Fanatic.

Beware the Solemn Believer — *praying is preying.*

ur   *plow*

In order to rebuild, to construct anew, to overcome & heal, the rubble of
war is always removed, but is absolute healing possible? Do wounds not
remain? When a scab falls away, is not the tissue still scarred, or *feel* as if it
is? Does it not carry memory of the scar? Think of the wound Genet says
each of us keeps within, *preserves*, and to which we withdraw in search of
solitude. Is the removal of all rubble not an act of erasure, an enactment
of oblivion?

> …German audiences were moved not long ago by the dra-
> matization of *The Diary of Anne Frank*. But even the ter-
> ror of the *Diary* has been an exceptional reminder. And
> it does not show what happened to Anne *inside* the camp.
> There is little market for such things in Germany. Forget
> the past. Work. Get prosperous. The new Germany belongs
> to the future. — George Steiner

What conscientious memorial can evoke disaster, or sustain the ever pres-
ent but submerged horrors imprinted in our cells, the lacerations that
remain in our cries, our whispers, our stuttering, our shrieking, even in
the act of lifting a spoon?

What if spaces of silence & destruction were preserved so as to perpetu-
ally maintain the presence of shatterings, of silence, with borders raised
around the rubble, the disaster, the destroyed form?

nulli sua forma manebat
obstabatque aliis aliud, quia corpore in uno
frigida pugnabant calidis, umentia siccis,
mollia cum duris, sine pondere habentia pondus

     chaos: rudis indigestaque moles
nec quicquam nisi pondus iners congestaque eodem
non bene iunctarum discordia semina rerum

sic erat instabilis tellus, innabilis unda,
lucis egens aer.....

Yet, what of the danger, the eventual banalization of chaos, of disaster's neutralization? Is the impact of *Salò* denuded with each screening, or is it truly indigestible? Would the power of such a work not be sustained if it were kept from mass distribution and its presentation ritualized? How can we sustain the viscerality and force, the ferocity & terror, of spaces of destruction? How to evoke true devastation? How to make chaos perpetually dynamic? With sounds; with every dimension of destruction; with putrid scents? Instead of an eternal flame, what of a chimney of intermittently burning flesh? What of nerve-excoriating images that haphazardly sear us as we walk the streets? What of devastating, absolute silences; the total evaporation of sound; the evaporation of even the heartbeat, of the pulse, of the noise of the nervous system?

Let us sustain such spaces, and in the midst of the new, to let disaster always perpetually hover before us, in all of our public squares — not heroic statues, not conscientious memorials, not comforting monuments, *but spaces of silence & destruction, spaces of disaster*. Is this not each civilization's question mark? History is always forgotten because we erase it when the blood of the soil should pulsate or erupt from the ground randomly, as shrieks, howls, scents of disaster. The disturbing dread of true silence; the silence of infinite spaces. All forms of terror must be present. Let us be eternally haunted, terrified, by history's phantoms. "Life" is not good as the infinitely myopic naively utter in wanton idiocy (to reflect more honestly their solipsism, they should say: "*my* life is great," or : "life is great *for me*"), or as the superficial Dionysians believe, they who think they are devoid of nihilism. All of the most destructive, violent forces pervade us — every cell, every rock, even the mote.

Memorials are to be destroyed. Spaces of Silence & Destruction must have greater force, be more unsettling than horror films.

ERASURE..AMNES

Quand s'ébranla le barrage de l'homme, aspiré par la faille géante de l'abandon du divin, des mots dans le lointain, des mots qui ne voulaient pas se perdre, tentèrent de résister à l'exorbitante poussée. Là se décida la dynastie de leur sens.

René Char, *Le poème pulvérisé*

GÉRARD DE NERVAL

22 May 1808 – 26 January 1855
rue de la Vieille-Lanterne, 1e

22 May 2015 — 13h30

The death of God has left a number of dark doors opening on to the void… — so said he who, decades before Rimbaud, proclaimed *Je suis l'autre*, and who, on 26 January 1955, traversed who knows what ſtreets, passages, alleys, *&* impasses, turned through who knows what number of dark doors, before turning here, to this final place of erasure, to this final void.

Gautier observed that Nerval took pleasure in disappearing from himself, in vanishing even from his work, and here, before one of the dark doors that had been opened with our emancipation from the onto-theological empire, Nerval vanished yet again, with extreme prejudice, with terrible violence, seeking an absolute invisibility, disappearing from himself forever, as he could only once more, on a ſtreet that would no less itself eventually also disappear, be erased from the grid of Paris and exiſt thereafter only in old maps, in engravings, in letters and news reports, in the imaginary of literary hiſtory.

Our witnesses: the gargoyles of Tour Saint-Jacques, golden-winged Victory of the Fontaine du Palmier, the Seine, *&* the dark black sky of that cold night, if not to mention the billions of ſtars, the nebulæ, the quasars, the not-yet discovered dark matter — whether visible or not, each remain present, felt, sensed, *there*, juſt as we have always been in their midſt, here in ſpace.

Having ſtretched his thread as far as he could bear to ſtretch it, teſting it in ever novel ways, extending it across centuries and continents, across cultures *&* civilizations, across psychic and literal terrain, all of which he embodied and reconfigured, him being the self-proclaimed son of Napoleon's brother,

Nerva, & Otho, it severed, he severed it, let the tautness go slack as he tied a rope to his neck and — *snap*, loosened the tension, one final spasm, his thread swiftly unraveling before all those witnesses, like intestines surging out of a gutted pig …

Le Nègres of Dumas, ⅓ Gérard, the interregnum: O Gérard Labrunie, O Orlando, O he who was once Gérard and still is, O M. Personne, can we rightfully, legitimately, & with any sense, ask, who were "you," *tu, l'autre?* What would *tu* make of the name of the street that is now closest to the one where you severed the thread: rue Adolphe Adam? *O Holy Night?* He clearly did not possess your lucidity. And what would you make of what has become of the places where you last breathed? Now the Théâtre de la Ville and, of all things, the Préfecture de Police. Nerval, a vagrant, Nerval, homeless, Nerval, dead before dying, pursued by the police, by creditors, by mockers, but not then by the public, you who were just as much all the names in history, you who penned farewells as cryptic, logical, & elegant as Herr Dynamite's:

Il fait si beau que l'on ne peut se rencontrer ni s'embrasser dans les maisons. Je vais tâcher de revenir.

Addio,
Il cav. G. Nap. della torre Brunya

With stoic indifference one could say that Goethe's praise was sufficient. Forget the roaring din, forget the teeming throng, forget the reviews which have such power that they threaten and undermine in the long defining moment but which years later are forgotten, as those who wrote them, save to the cataloguers and accountants of literary history. Can we imagine you in the ridiculous position of having to be a professor? What else more could one need than Goethe's blessing? But more is needed, and one must live. How does a poet survive, persist, flourish?

Gonzalo: Here is everything advantageous to life.
Antonio: True; save means to live.
Sebastian: Of that there's none, or little.

                        Is it possible to stand here
now, to look out upon the external world, 160 years later, and consider
it real? Is not your *généalogie fantastique* more real in its lucid irreality?
Is that year not the year that you first died, or did you first die as a *nègres*
of Dumas, your name erased, ridiculed, a ghost before a god? Or did
you die yet earlier, and were you perhaps always dead, only at last giv-
ing birth to yourself on that final day, in the darkness of the rue de la
Vieille-Lanterne, Victory's arms reaching out, her wings stretched back,
her head poised to the future? Toward you, no wing. What did you
think of as you gazed at her, or at the nearby gargoyles? Did she know
gargoyles were in hot pursuit of you, their teeth growing ever sharper
with each advance? Baudelaire said you delivered your soul in the dark-
est street that you could find. It was as if you knew it would vanish soon
after you died, and so it was, demolished the very same year of your
own auto-demolition. The teeth of the gargoyles devoured you. In their
stillness, you were immobilized, made more silent than a statue, more
invisible than an atom.

        What are we to make of this name, whose irony
in relation to you is too obvious to articulate? Rue de la Vieille-Lanterne.
Does it recall Diogenes, and were you not for so long like one who carries
a lantern in the daytime? Does one like you, who has lived at so many
addresses, and who has undergone so many interrogations, so many hos-
pitalizations, even exist at all? I am certain a **(t)koimo-* was not some-
thing you knew, though perhaps briefly, during those last years in Passy.
No, it was mostly the *Unheimlich* that you knew. Were you too suicided
by society?

        The same violent death you brought against your fictional
alter egos, deaths delivered by their doppelgangers, by their *autres*, that
same severing of the thread, the final half of *Aurelia* in your jacket pocket

— however different the circumstances, one cannot without pause think also of Radnóti & his last march … —, your hat still on your head, here, in what is now a stage, yet one which does not perform your dramas — the sirens sound again, the *schrei* of the ambulances, nearly 200 years too late, sounding in the future for the dead poet — here, your death, a mythic founding event out of which a world could be created, *a mythos of poets*, here, a theater is built upon this site as a church was built upon the site of St. Peter's body. Is that the secret & actual hermetic truth behind the construction of the theater? Is your body perhaps there, beneath the footlights, not in Père Lachaise, in that crowded grave?

Here, in the void, before several now open doors, as the sun bears down upon me, and more sirens resound, here, in this void that is a darkness even in the sun, your name does not exist. No plaque, no sign, no sculpture — — only a void. Rue *Adolphe Adam*, not rue Gérard Nerval. Of what significance though is a street name?

Perhaps that void is you and you are here, in this absence, in this *mise en abyme*, the spire of Notre Dame in the distance, the clouds, the interregnum that you opened, the darkest darkness, the final manuscript, the final words, the *Innigkeit*, le *Soleil noir de la Mélancolie* …

Is this where our monument to poets should be built? Does a monument not exist at every site where every poet has sacrificed himself?

Nothing could be constructed here in your honor except this invisibility, wandering between two words, one dead, the other powerless to be born. But is this intensified invisibility sufficient to stand against *tours* such as the Eiffel? If the invisible is only visible to the initiate, is its vital impact not lost? The initiates are not the ones in need …

Luca would come to confront this truth over 100 years later, and we confront it today as the hammers of ISIS shatter what poets like you sought to establish, as the book is under threat and extinction, as the poet remains an anomaly before the blitzkrieg of the 21ˢᵗ-century spectacle of inanity and banality, of vacuity. Would the life of the poet make for "reality television"? Will Asclepius save us from Hippocrates? Have we any right to hope? Is such hope not a form of madness, or, *stupidity*? Has not Anesidora suffocated hope in her pithos?

You, the non-existent other, son of Napoleon's brother, you who severed the thread not as Deleuze, but as Luca *&* Celan, you who made the night black and white, did you gaze out across the Seine and see these prison-like windows and this little green door that is the abode of some enigmatic figure? Did you see it as the prison of the poet? It was to the sky that you gave yourself, and the night, the darkness, the dark matter that you did not know but which you felt, as the thread slackened within you and scuttled in your body with terrible lacerating force, a snake coursing through your guts till everything within you had turned to venom and, seeking to be born, you severed the thread, birth pangs convulsing your body as it twitches before Victory and the Tour Saint-Jacques, its gargoyles snarling over the abyss, jutting into the darkness like flick-blades: — *snap snap snap…*

Is that not ironic, too? Did the *tour* inspire Dumas to write *La tour Saint-Jacques*, or was it not *tu*? Is it his silent homage, knowing as he did of your bond with Nicolas Flamel, more, *knowing his injustices*?

In 1858, only three years later, sphinxes would accompany Victory, sphinxes made to commemorate the triumph of your uncle in Egypt. Was it not actually à *toi* also that those sphinxes were commemorated? Or not also, *but only*, and *truly*? For what more perfect figures could there be to honor you with? Is not the poet the sphinx *par excellence*? Was this an act of the initiates? Is this another hermetic secret?

I commemorate them to you. Let us call them the Sphinxes of Nerval. Or let us give each one of them a different name, as you so named your selves. They are not the

Sphinxes of Nerval, they are Nervals in & of them selves, each of them
a lantern in the daylight, each of them the darkness of the light.

Art is not worth this to me; farewell, my aulos.

Krankhaft!

PROHIBITION? TRANSFORMATION

Animation of art. — Art raises its head where religions subside. It takes over a host of moods and feelings engendered by religion, lays them to its heart, and itself grows more profound, more soulful, so that it is now capable of communicating exultation and enthusiasm as it formerly could not. The wealth of religious feelings, swollen to a torrent, breaks forth again and again and seeks to conquer new regions: but the growth of the Enlightenment undermined the dogmas of religion and infused a fundamental mistrust of them: so that the feelings expelled from the sphere of religion by the Enlightenment throw themselves into art; in some cases into political life as well, even straight into the sciences. Wherever we perceive human endeavors to be tinted with a higher, gloomier coloring, we can suspect that dread of spirits, the odor of incense and the shadows of churches are still adhering to them.

Nietzsche

And so, during battle, Mongol invaders destroy the House of Wisdom of Baghdad, Iraq. And they murder Euclid and Ptolemy, Persians,
Indians, and Greeks, and Mohammed ibn Musa al-Khwarizmi, too,
drowning them all, asphyxiating them in a river, as they asphyxiate the
library of Ibh Hiban & the qadi of Nishapur, spating them into oblivion.

*O words, O dangerous words, O numbers, O dangerous numbers, flow on,
turn the Tigris black, make the river ink, a torrent of wisdom & knowledge,
turn back into that from which you came.*

Beware the Book?
Beware the Purifiers!
Beware Libricide.

Art is a sublime mission
that necessitates fanaticism.

Adolf Hitler

Lire, écrire, comme on vit sous la surveillance du désastre : exposé à la passivité hors passion. L'exaltation de l'oubli.

Ce n'est pas toi qui parleras ; laisse le désastre parler en toi, fût-ce par oubli ou par silence.

Maurice Blanchot, *L'Écriture du désastre*

And so, during the Spanish occupation of Granada, instead of giving pearls to pigs, Cardinal Ximenes incinerates every Arabic manuscript in Granada — a public bonfire, the écrasez of the Alpujarras, the churching of mosques, the refusal of polytheism. Baptism, or exile — monotheism demands fire.

Beware the Book?

Beware the *klasmos* cardinals.

The project of immortality
will forever fail
because it is DE-VOID
of agonistic tension — —

each & every metaphysic
is an anti-physic
an anti-phusis

There are still prophets, & believers in them?
Every prophet must abandon his god for the earth
Every prophet must suffer shattering
undergo the great abdication
& be transformed
as

became Triboulet

Allah too must become a

As kings once did, every religion needs a fool!

Now the sirens have a still more fatal weapon than their song, namely their

SILENCE

And though admittedly such a thing has never happened, still it is con-
ceivable that someone might possibly have escaped from their singing;
but from their silence certainly

NEVER

Kafka

Is enduring the shattering force
A QUESTION
of Democritean vs. Heraclitean perspectives,
or would certain events make even Democritus weep,
break him,
silence even his raucous,
Olympian laughter?

Is Zarathustra's laughing
at tragedies & tragic wakes
ever possible?
Can humans become *Übermenschen?*
Is the Eternal Return not the cleanest, most lucid theodicy?

Has not the pathway into the future been foreseen?
The structure, the praxis, the *askeses*
for an anti-metaphysical theodicy
rest in this alone.

What too of the *sub specie æternitatis* perspective?

Some are crushed by events,
paralyzed,
deadened,
Still yet others rise & continue ~

There is no salvation,
there is no redemption:

TIME PROCEEDS WITHOUT MERCY
as elusive as the kairos,
as ferocious as Saturn.
Yet, are there figures that can make of even the Eternal Return
a hurdy-gurdy?

One formerly devoted to logos, now silent, mentally paralyzed, his self having fragmented, his former works, *sundered by words.*

Rhetoric is now to him but a carapace, a skein distinct from atoms. An abyss stands before him *&* logos: words putrefy in his mouth, undergo *transfiguration,* fuse, then shatter *&* encircle him, mutate into staring eyes into which he stares back.

Ancient Greek *&* Roman texts no longer invigorate him; before them, he feels as if imprisoned in a garden rife with insensate statues. Only simple, concrete things affect his nerves.

Emptiness now rules, and it is not cantatas, madrigals, or triptychs, but only crickets, autumn winds, and howling dogs that are the sources of mysterious, wordless, infinite rapture. Like Crassus, he weeps over the death of eels.

His thinking is pyrexiac, more unmediated, molten, *&* fervent than words. He proclaims that he will not write books in any known language. He thinks in a wordless tongue, one in which the voiceless speaks. Perhaps, he says, when I am dead, I will have something to say.

Writerdom is a race with a revolting smell to its hide and the filthiest known means of preparing its food. It is a race that wanders and sleeps in its own vomit, one that is expelled from cities and hounded in villages, but it is always & everywhere close to the authorities, who grant them a place in red-light districts, as prostitutes. For literature always & everywhere carries out one assignment: it helps superiors keep their soldiers obedient and it helps judges execute reprisals against doomed men.

A writer is a mixture of parrot & pope.

Osip Mandelstam

Words have killed images or are concealing them. A civilization of words is a civilization distraught. Words create confusion. Words are not the word ... The fact is that words say nothing, if I may put it that way...

Ionesco

And so, in Glasney, Penryn, Cornwall, Royal Officials smash & loot the Cornish Colleges — scriptoria destroyed! Cornish language, Cornish cultural identity, obliterated.

The dissolution of the monasteries, the dissolution of culture, the subsidization of war:

A great parte of the Leade that covereth the saide Chuch by virtue of warrant from the Counsell was sent to the thiles of Sille for the Kings Maiesties fortificacions there ...

All Hail English, All Hail the Liturgy!

Beware the Book?

Beware the Vicar-General.

Beware the Iconoclasts.

Not long after, Renato returns to Paris, and for the first time since leaving Berlin, he has his own room, regains his privacy, though not true isolation, for his room has no door, only a curtain, and, in myriad ways, his room-mates perforate and transude him, frequently entering his room when he is not present, making him feel that his body has no dimension, that even the border or boundary of his skin doesn't exist, while scents and sounds become invasive to him, contagions that enter him against his will, breaking through the geo-tertium quid of his corpus and dissipating him.

> *La plus dangereuse des invasions, l'invasion de la vie intérieure, est infiniment plus dangereuse qu'une invasion ou occupation territoriale.* — Ch. Péguy

Excited to be in the city, to bring an end to the long suspension of his life, he retrieves his belongings and begins settling in, lining the half-empty shelves in the room with the few books he has retained. As the days go by, he wanders through the streets, exploring new quartiers, cafes, and parts of Paris he has never visited, haunting the cinemas and gardens and bookstores, the desire to read slowly beginning to form within him, a root starting to bud, a stillness, a silence, a necessary solitude, even if compromised.

Two weeks later, to his delight, a friend has a reading chair delivered to his apt. When Renato sits in it, to his great shock, & without any sense that it is about to occur, the thread begins to unwind: — he weeps, trembles, is overcome by powerful emotions, tears rush from out his ducts.

He begins to feel disoriented, not entirely himself, as if on the verge of some radical dissociation, like a loosely spun spool of thread that may rapidly unravel or spin into a mass of chaotic skeins. His insides feel like loose material in a state of constant fluctuation. There is no inner coherence.

Unsettled, deeply ill at ease, he suffers strong, intense oscillations of mood
constantly.

*   *   *   *   *

.... can't write, too discombobulated
fragmented
lack of coherence
       stability — *Ganzheit*

disassociation
spiral into oblivion
seeming to reconstitute, but only temporarily

sounds........voices *grate*
EXPOSURE
bereft of library, bereft of true solitude
bereft of existence

*   *   *   *   *

I hear the ruin of all space, shattered glass and toppling masonry,
and time one livid final flame. What's left us then?

c o

t nes t

The name of God should no longer come from the mouth of man.
This word, for so long degraded by use, no longer means anything.
It is devoid of

meaning
of all blood....

words,

immortal,
invulnerable...

suffer...

incurable....

These guardians of meaning,
are not

Like men, words

Some may survive, others are

In the night everything is confused,

there are

no more names

no more forms

Adamov, *The Confession* (1938)

And so, during the Conquest of the Americas, by order of Bishop Diego de Landa in July of 1652, Catholics destroy the works of the Yucatan.

The Indigenous must be cleansed of Satan.

We found a large number of books in these characters and, as they contained nothing in which were not to be seen as superstition and lies of the devil, we burned them all, which the Maya regretted to an amazing degree, and which caused them much affliction.

Beware the Book?

Beware the Exorcists. Or, as one exulted:

May these bishops expiate their crimes
in the Purgatory of Biblioclasts!

Here, close to the Mango Grove of Pavarika, the Buddha gives sermons.

The ridgepoles of each monk's chamber are carved with dragons, the beams painted in variegated colors. The supporting beam of the structure is green, the pillars crimson. The frontal columns and railings of each chamber have ornamental engravings and hollowed-out carvings. The plinths are of jade, the rafter tips covered with drawings. Silk pennants hang from ropes connecting the eves.

The monks study the Hindu Vedas, logic, Sanskrit grammar, medicine, and divination. For food they eat areca nuts, nutmeg, non-glutinous rice, and butter and milk. They burn incense; they chew betel leaves.

In 1193, Turkish Muslims invade Central Bihar. At the University Complex, Bakhtivar Khalji asks, *Is there a Koran here?*

At his behest, the invaders destroy the place that confers the lotus, one of the most renowned repositories of Buddhist knowledge in the world. Nearly 1700 years after having been founded, it is almost entirely reduced to rubble.

The monks flee to Tibet. Those who remain die under the sword. Temples & monasteries are decimated, too.

The biblioclasm shatters the development of the sciences of anatomy, astronomy, alchemy, & mathematics in ancient India.

Al-la-hu ak-bar. Wu-sha-fa.

From the mosque in Bamiyan, charges are detonated.

Destruction:

Al-laahh, ha!
Al-la-hu ak-bar. Al-la-hu ak-bar.
Al-la-hu ak-bar. Al-la-hu ak-bar.
Al-la-hu ak-bar.
Wu-sha-fa.
Al-laahh!!

The firing of weapons in the air.
Euffant dancing.
The sacrifice of nine cows.

العمل يؤدي إلى الحرية..

Arbeit Macht Frei?

Paris, Pont Mirabeau, XVe
23 November 2015: midnight

From where, if this is the exact locale, did he leap? At the edge of the bridge; at the center; or elsewhere? And at what time — in the morning, before sunrise, at night, when the light of the sun is darkened by the moon, or at some other moment? And was he seen? Was there a witness who was in accord with his act, who embraced it as one of his or her own (desire) but one he or she was not strong enough to commit? A witness who chose not to intervene in the poet's act, one which perhaps conveyed some sense of relief, or which slackened the thread, enabling them to continue for another day, week, month … or hour.

What happens to a Russian or a Czech does not interest me in the slightest. Whether these nations live in prosperity or starve to death interest me only insofar as we need them as slaves for our Kultur. Whether ten thousand Russian females fall down dead from exhaustion while digging an anti-tank ditch interests me only insofar as the anti-tank ditch for Germany is finished. We Germans, who are the only people in the world who have a decent attitude towards animals, will also assume a decent attitude towards those human animals, but it is a crime against our own blood to worry about them or give them ideals. — Himmler

Did he see birds as I now see them, standing here in distant (non)-communication? Was there wind, like now? Silence? Or the gentle rustling noise of the end of the night; the creaking of boat ropes, of bows rising and falling, delicately breaking the water's surface, a series of shock waves breaking into the depths with each plunge? Did he think of 1940 & Russia, of 1942 & Germany, of herding and of camps? Did he think of Goll, of his books burning?

From here, from this point at the center of the bridge, where I now stand, if he stood at this point and leapt from it, one can see both the Statue de la Liberté & La Tour Eiffel. Freedom. Industry. The first figure is 11.50 meters high, the second, 300.65 meters.

How many times did he cross this bridge and contemplate absolute silence? Or walk along the Seine while contemplating it? In gazing upon this juxtaposition, of liberty dwarfed by industry, what pressure did it exert upon him? Was it a breaking weight? There is no causal relation; other more exacting knives cut into his flesh, whittled the thread bare in his search for reality.

Or did he surreptitiously, silently, calmly enter the water from below the bridge, closer to the surface of the river, arriving noiselessly, gently, not plunging — a soft, delicate violence. Did he weigh himself down so that he would sink to the depths and not be able to rise, or did he swim first, then slowly descend, breathturn by breathturn, holding out till his lungs could no longer resist, the water suffusing his lungs, his body convulsing, jerking, twitching against the force, fighting the snapping of the thread, but not having enough counter pressure to do so — it had been worn thin, frayed, stripped of its filaments by agony, memory, emotion, torment, all infinitesimally lacerating it, neutron by neutron, atom by atom, neuron by neuron, hair by hair, cell by cell, till the anvil could bear no more duress, till even iron cracked. Do you hear Apollo sharpening his blade?

Or maybe he turned and leapt from the other direction, away from the dwarfing of liberty, toward a less exacting

nothingness, toward a neutrality and negation even more cold & brutal,
like the negation of history, of the implacable pressure & incisiveness of
the real being deemed surreal, his thread, as his poetry, growing more bro-
ken, language growing as shattered as his self — each condensed, shorn
of locale, *lessened,* scaled to a sharp brevity, tightened & tightened like
a violin string, denude of metrics, denude of syntactic elements, each a
series of breaths grown briefer and briefer, proceeding toward negation:

> *he speaks truly who speaks the shade*

        Edging toward the precipice of
his inner citadel, pivoting upon a narrower & narrower arc, entering the
ambiguous realm of the amorphous field of forces that constitute the self,
an enigma, that which is unspeakable, the ashen light before the storm,
the shattering of clocks, of calendars, and art as an obdurate conundrum,
as that which exists in silence, or incomprehension, as it awaits a word
which cuts the thread, which cut it for him:

> *vielleicht geht die Dichtung,*
> *wie die Kunst, mit einem*
> *selbstvergessenen Ich zu jenem*
> *Unheimlichen und Fremden,*
> *und setz sich — doch wo? doch*
> *an welchem Ort? doch womit?*
> *doch als was? — wieder frei?*

        Can one exist as an estranged *subjectum* for whom the
sky is an abyss? Or does this path lead to a terrifying silence which en-
gulfs the breath and which engulfs language, like water filling the lungs?
Is the turn of the breath ultimately a turn toward death? A turn with a
threatening pause or *suspension* of breath, a turn toward a void, or oblit-
erating dark matter? There is the silence between words, the silence be-
tween notes, and there is the ultimate and absolute silence, the silence
of shattering, of the still-here breaking down into the already-no-more,
poetry becoming catastrophe, existence not balancing on the abyss but

descending into it, not returning home & hovering in proximity to death or *alogos*, but moving beyond, into an irreparable realm, into a volcano, a tower, a river, a terrace. Was it the 'failure' of purifying German that also whittled the thread to bits, stripped him of his skin? The *à rebours* word as the counterword; the counterword that breaks the word; the fall into silence; the severing diaphragm spasm; the breaking of the psalms; the breaking of the lyre. Hopes & promises negated; the lyric negated; optimism negated; redemption nullified. Art questioned; poetry questioned; logos questioned. Burrowing into narrows; thresholds ever more perilously approached; threadsuns woven by the Fates, in Hyperborea, north of the future where poetry measures space, where poetry wields the burden of measuring even the *Khurbn*, what is beyond understanding, beyond the Unknown which comes to live in the poet, beyond the breath, beyond the rhythm that is mute thought shaping respiration, a thought which expired breathturn by breathturn, winding from the Seine to the Cimetière parisien de Thiais, the apocalyptic star not glittering, *but genius going dark, sinking into the bitter well of the heart*, near, in the aorta's arch, in bright blood: the brightword.

Art is not worth this to me; farewell, my aulos.

𝕶rankhaft!

There is that terrible being
                         staring in contemplation
                         his mouth agape
                                   him pivoting anxiously
                                   as if about to *flee*
s\pli/t   between   d i r e c t ~~~~~ i o n s
                         his vision
           o   v   e   r   a   r   c   h   i   n   g
           ours —   sh-a-t-te-red

before the ceaselessly accumulating wreckage
                         to remain,
                         to take what has been sh-a-t-te-red,
                         to achieve *Ganzheit,*
           that is his desire,
yet a storm impedes his movement
           [—immobilizes him—]
                                   thrusts him a-gainst his path
casting him
backwards
& as he gazes toward another destination
the
wreck
age
con
tin
ues
to
a
c
cu
mu
late

PROHIBITION!

"What is this principle of party literature? It is not simply that, for the socialist proletariat, literature cannot be a means of enriching individuals or groups, but that it cannot be an individual undertaking at all, independent of the general proletarian cause. Down with non-party writers! Down with literary supermen! The literary business has to become *part* of the general proletarian business, a 'little wheel and little screw' of the single and united great Social Democratic mechanism, set in motion by all the conscious avant-garde of the working class. Literary business has to become an integral part of the organized, planned united Social Democratic Party work."

Lenin

I'm not a worker. I grow wilder with each passing day.
— Mandelstam

Carte
Ethnographique
L'Europe

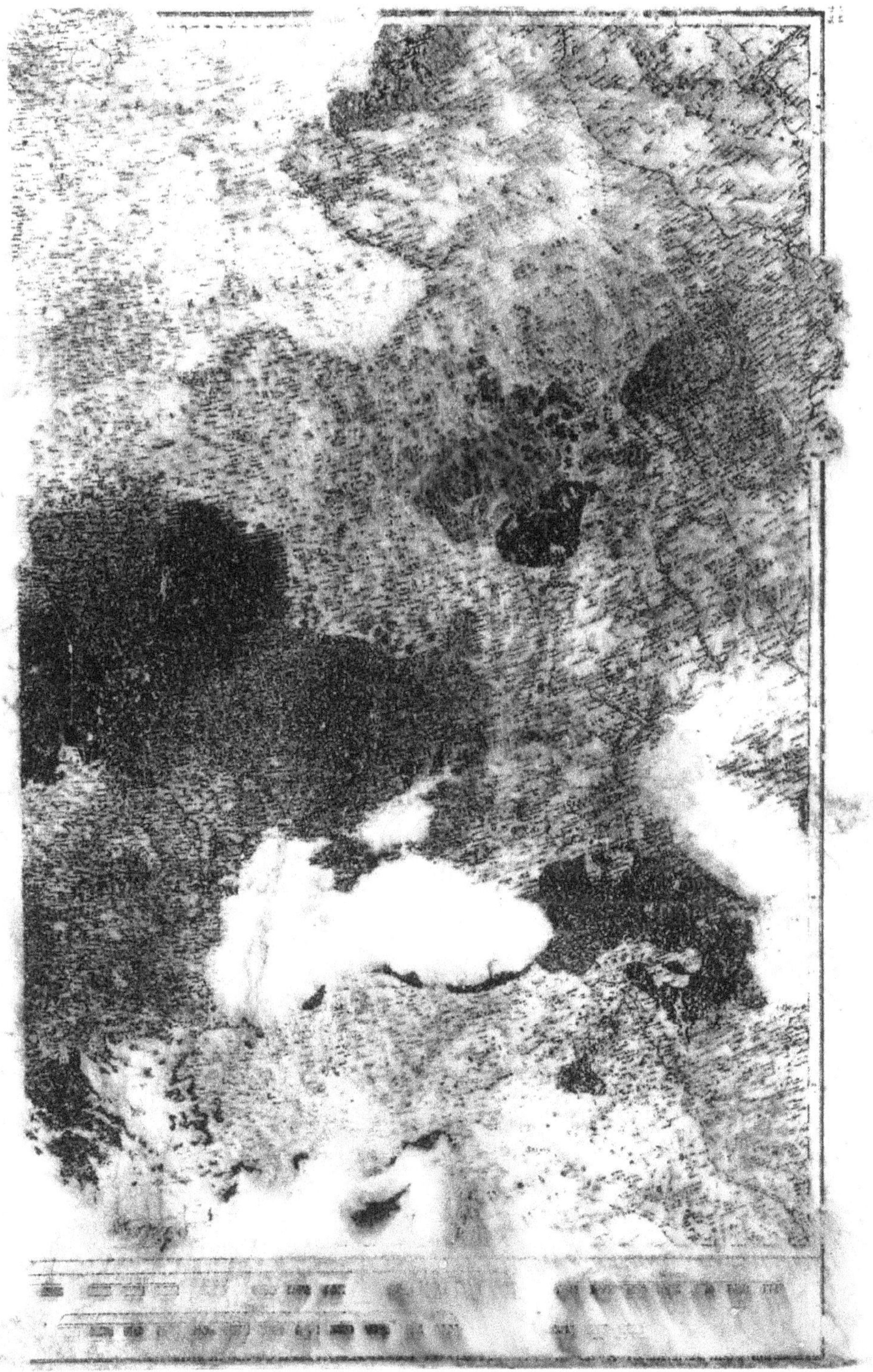

And so, in 1790, upon suppression of country monasteries, 25,000 Catholic manuscripts & over 4 million books are burned in France thruout the century.

Beware the Book?

Beware the Reformers.

Denn *dass der Mensch erlöst werde von der Rache*: das ist mir
die Brücke zur höchsten Hoffnung und ein Regenbogen nach langen
Unwettern.

Friedrich Nietzsche
Also sprach Zarathustra

I, your servant, propose that all historians' records other than those of Qin's be burned. With the exception of the academics whose duty includes possessing books, if anyone under heaven has copies of the Shi Jing, the Classic of History, or the writings of the hundred schools of philosophy, they shall deliver them to the governor or the commandant for burning. Anyone who dares to discuss the Shi Jing, the Classic of History shall be publicly executed. Anyone who uses history to criticize the present shall have his family executed. Any official who sees the violations but fails to report them is equally guilty. Anyone who has failed to burn the books after thirty days of this announcement shall be subjected to tattooing and be sent to build the Great Wall. The books that have exemption are those on medicine, divination, agriculture, and forestry. Those who have interest in laws shall instead study from officials. — Chancellor Li Si

Poetry, history, and philosophy
are works of subversion
and to be destroyed.

In 206 BC, the Qin Imperial Palaces are burned

  the archives laid to waste
   in burning pits;

     each flame
     each wisp of smoke
     each crumbling flake of ash —

       WORDS
       LETTERS
       INCINERATED THOUGHT

       Burning pits of ignorance

工作使你自由...

In 210 BC, the Qin Shi Huangdi orders
                              the live burial
                              AT XIANYANG
                              of 460 Confucian scholars,
                              some say nearly 1200

Other scholars are exiled to the extremities of the country.

Thought is buried; thought is exiled.

To exterminate them is to exterminate œuvre upon œuvre.
                              To commit *human biblioclasms* —

                              the flesh
                              like paper
                              burning too;
                              the book of the body,
                              burning…

R
P
F

We are issuing this manifesto of ruinous and incendiary violence, by which we today are founding Futurism, because we want to deliver Italy from its gangrene of professors, archaeologists, tourist guides and antiquaries.

Italy has been too long the great second-hand market. We want to get rid of the innumerable museums that cover it with innumerable cemeteries.

Let the good incendiaries with charred fingers come! Here they are! Heap up the fire to the shelves of the libraries! Divert the canals to flood the cellars of the museums! Let the glorious swim ashore! Take the picks and hammers! Undermine the foundation of venerable towns!

We want to glorify war — the only cure for the world — militarism, patriotism, the destructive gesture of the anarchists, the beautiful ideas which kill, and contempt for woman.

Museums, cemeteries!

Marinetti

And so, in 1870, during the Franco-Prussian War, the German Army
sets the Strasbourg Library on fire, destroying books and papers, includ-
ing the original lawsuit records of Johann Gutenberg vs. his partners.

Abandon all hope of knowing the history of the invention of print-
ing in the West.

Burn the papers of the printer!

Were you acolytes of Rousseau?

Beware the Book?

Beware the Marauders.

Man arrives at speech
out of the magnitude of his fear
of remaining
even one moment

                                                     in the abyss

face to face
with unmediated

                                  nothingness

Haim Nahmann Bialik

extreme sensitivity
    rawness — as if devoid of skin
        disquieted
      inner fracturing

inability   to   think
only disjointed phrases come

frequently collapse
spells of incomprehensible weeping

collusions, similar acts, of friends, others   ? ?

when people come too close to me in the street, invade the hemisphere
of my body, I have the urge to attack them... to lash out, to cold-
cock them for invading the boundary, to ferociously thrash them.
DON'T WALK SO FUCKING CLOSE POTA DE CRISTO

*   *   *   *   *

The 'person' is decomposing. Others see only the phantasm of the mask,
lack awareness of the unconscious dissimulation. There is no determinate
physiognomy, only the semblance of it, the persona, that which the seem-
ing person sounds through, the *phersu*. What was unforeseeable and un-
fathomable has burst forth; a limit-point has been reached; crossed over.

His protective citadel gone, he is exposed. *(Chaos prevails* ... The vacancy
of the conscious ego.

The I that signed itself Renato barely exists. I — there is something
absurd in saying it, 'he' says to 'himself'... There is only impulse and fluc-
tuation, a violent discombobulation of the tonalities of the soul.

Will restoration occur, or will there be a violent dispersion, a sparagmos?
Contact, normal congress, has been constricted, for the regular words &
gestures of the individual Renato have been narrowed. He has been split
into too many pieces, over too great a terrain. In honor of an ethic, he has
erased himself. A mirror has been shattered. Only the arbitrary prevails,
the unknowable. What is left of the self may merge with chaos & forever
obliterate he who was once known as Renato.

Is this some form of destructive plasticity? A possible annihilating meta-
morphosis? If absence and exile constitute the only presence, are they ...
sustaining?

*   *   *   *   *

After hanging my — *this vacant fucking word* ... leather jacket on the wall,
deep disquiet ... Gazing at it in terror: a coat is not visible, but *a dangling
shell of skin*, like the loose bag of flesh in Meier's *Apollo & Marsyas*, or
Amusco's *Historia de la composicion del cuerpo humano*. Felt as if it was
my removed skin & there Renato was, exposed, vulnerable, not a living
being, but, *an anatomy object. A specimen.*

*   *   *   *   *

Renato is a ball of feeling points and everything presses upon him &
him on everything.

    severer chaos of a mind untun'd —

The word not only brings things out of silence; it also produces the silence in which they can disappear again.

Max Picard, *The World of Silence*

And so, in 1871, blackened paper, debris from the city archives, wafts thru the air, floating thru the streets of Paris, drifting even to the *banlieues* and beyond, and at nine in the evening, fires rise in the air as the Tuileries erupt in flames, the fire consuming the entire building, which was smeared in petroleum.

The guardians of the Louvre are taken hostage and threatened with execution.

Days later, an explosion shakes the Louvre to its foundations — the palace is transformed into a furnace of colorful flames, provoked by the mineral oils and other ingredients at the heart of the burning fire. The Library of the Louvre is destroyed, and the Tuileries smolder for days.

When learning of the conflagrations, Nietzsche went in search of Burckhardt, who himself went in search of Nietzsche, and once they finally found one another, for over an hour, at Nietzsche's table, they discussed the fate of European culture, the onslaught on the cultural continuity of *Alteuropa*, and the new manifestation of destructive energies originally engendered by the French Revolution.

Burckhardt: *Petroleum in the cellars of the Louvre and the flames in other palaces are an expression of what the Philosopher calls 'the will to live'; it is the last will and testament of mad fiends desiring to make a great impression on the world. The great harm was begun in the last century, mainly thru Rousseau, with his doctrine of the goodness of human nature.*

Nietzsche: *Over and above the struggle between nations, the object of our ter-
ror was that international hydra-head, suddenly and so terrifyingly appearing
as a sign of quite different struggles to come. In that phenomenon does our
modern life, actually the whole of old Christian Europe & its state, but, above
all, the "Romanic" civilization which is now everywhere predominant, show
the enormous degree to which our world has been damaged, and that, with all
our past behind us, we are all of us responsible for such terror coming to light,
so that we must make sure we do not ascribe to those unfortunates alone the
crime of fighting against culture. I know what it means, the fight against cul-
ture. When I heard of the fires in Paris, I felt for several days annihilated and
was overwhelmed by fears & doubts; the entire scholarly scientific, philosophi-
cal, & artistic existence seemed an absurdity, if a single day could wipe out
the most glorious works of art, even whole periods of art; I clung with earnest
conviction to the metaphysical value of art, which cannot exist for the sake of
poor human beings but which has higher missions to fulfill. But even when
the pain was at its worst, I could not cast a stone against those blasphemers,
who were to me only carriers of the general guilt…*

"Burn down the Louvre! All museums must be destroyed!"
— Apollinaire +

Many of them also, which used curious arts, brought their books together, and burned them before all men: and they counted the price of them, and found it fifty thousand pieces of silver.

— Acts 19:19

ONE THREAD
            continuously
            COMBATS
the other — —
            this is the exacting dialectic.
                        The superior power
                  of one
                              must   SHATTER
                  a-gain-st
the other

            DESTRUCTION
            COL-LAPSE
            DIS-ASTER : —
            these are not end forces
             but fundamental forces;
                  governing   forces;
                  &   each exist
                               within
                               the other.

To en-
act
the *Un*
ter
gang
is
to ex-
press
the most ultimate *amor fati*
            EXISTENCE
            is affirmed
         in the recognition
            of dis-aster
         of the SHATTERING
          of all creative acts
         in the gospel
            of failure

Nothing can be where the word fails.

Stefan George

GHERASIM LUCA
23 July 1913 – 9 February 1995
Pont Mirabeau, XVe

23 July 2015, 8:13 PM

Is there a tower built to poetry as imposing as the one built to industry?
I think of this as I think of Luca standing on this bridge, twenty-four
years after Celan, who stood here twenty-four years after Voronca, hav-
ing reached a threshold where the thread could no longer be kept taut. Is
there any tower or monument to art as grand, as sacrificed to, as given
over to labor by the tired, the hungry, the poor? A devotion to a force
by those it has destroyed — *poets*.

    In one sense, we have this, but it is an
invisible, hidden, dispersed monument. It is made of the bodies, the spir-
its, the spent threads of every true poet from Pindar to Luca, each stand-
ing against the wind as I now am, the wind blowing thru the arches of
the tower of industry, winds which could topple the miniature statue at
the end of the aptly named Île aux Cygnes, visible from le Pont Mirabeau,
a wind to which I now turn my back so as to gaze up at the crescent
moon, the light of lunacy, of the *mœnsœc*, the sharp, dead planet which at
this moment resembles a harvesting sickle. Here, under this sharp, scin-
tillating blade, Luca, quite deliberately, cut his thread just where it was
cut by three of his compatriots, each 24 years apart from one another.
How many unique ways are there of dying in verse?

    Here, on an icy Feb-
ruary night, the light of the moon dimmed by the lights of industry,
dimmed by the lights of cars and buses and motorcycles and *les flics*, as
they do now, in tandem with their sirens. The light, the soft deceiving
bronze glow of the Eiffel and its searchlight beam, shooting out into the
night as if searching for those not devoted to it, that light which shot
out over the sky as Luca cut his thread after 80 years of defiance, of exile,
of wandering, of dreaming, of standing in combat against the Œdipal
scalpel & for the erotic dream.

The monuments to poetry, or to poets, if we have them, what are they but posthumous laurels of scant value and scant worth, laurels more like leaden nooses, rings of invisibility, barbed wire crowns. What energies, what efforts, let's say it, what *capital* has been devoted to poetry, to make it as formidable a presence, one concretized with equal industry? If a society devoted as much of its taxes to poetry as it does to war, what new form of society might be born? Who could construct such an entity as a monument to poetry? What sculptor, what architect?

Liberty is nearly invisible, has been made almost transparent by the similar greenness of the river and the surrounding bridges, almost usurped by its base, which is equal if not greater in height than the statue itself. The wind blows hard now, the moon darkens, sharpening its edge…

Did Luca think of Cendrars and Delaunay and their *Prose of the Trans-Siberian* which, if each copy were set atop the other, would equal the height of the Eiffel Tower? A monument to poiesis, to creation, mimicking, mocking, parodying the Eiffel.

The sirens screech out again, repeating their rhythm, a rhythm not as rich, not as urgent even, not as *impassioned* as Luca's rhythm, nor his incantations, each of which were considered an event by Deleuze while to Andre Velter, Luca rediscovered the oracular power of poetry *&* its virtue of subversion.

And what is this, what magnitude does this have; is it force enough to combat the reality principle? Is it sufficient? How many more poets will cut the thread like Luca? The night darkens, the edge grows ever sharper, the wind blows ever harder, as if to refuse even this memorial, this recollection, this meditation; as if to silence it, as the lights of industry silence the lights of the moon. Planetary light dimmed *&* darkened, obscured *&* occluded, by electric light.

Here he stood, thinking of Celan and of Voronca, the pressure having reached its final point of tensility, the blade of the moon slitting Luca's thread as he leapt into the Seine, closing a 74-year triangle, or opening another —

Do we hear the Andalusian dogs howling as their eyes are slit with razor blades? Can we hear their howling above the roar of the wind and the din of the city? Do we hear the splash of the poet's body as it hits the water and descends, its thread severed as the search-light shoots out and above, its light continuing to shine brightly as another light of the moon, that bright dead planet, is diffused? As now, by the almost mocking, glittering, sparkling lights that blind and twinkle off le Tour Eiffel like gaudy Christmas trinkets — a poet severed the thread. As these lights sparkle & scream, no light is visible from liberty's torch, only, just barely, the lights of her crown, but they too are diffused by the great beaming power of the Eiffel, which stretches far into every distance, circling all of Paris, from east to south to north to worstward as the thread of the *juif* disappears in the Seine, engulfed by the night, as invisible as his grave.

Art is not worth this to me; farewell, my aulos.

Madness Becomes Method!

On the Spoken Word all the gods depend, all beasts & men; in the
Word live all creatures; in the Word is the Imperishable, the firstborn of
the Eternal Law, the Mother of the Vedas, the navel of the divine world.

Taittiriya Brahmana

Let poets have the privilege and license to annihilate themselves.
To save a man against his will is as bad as to murder him.

Horace

To the Fates

One summer only grant me, you powerful Fates,
And one more autumn only for mellow song,
So that more willingly, replete with
Music's late sweetness, my heart may die then.

The soul in life denied its god-given right
        Down there in Orcus also will find no peace;
                But when what's holy, dear to me, the
                        Poem's accomplished, my art perfected,

Then welcome, silence, welcome cold world of shades!
        I'll be content, though here I must leave my lyre
                And songless travel down, for once I
                        Lived like the gods, and no more is needed.

                Hölderlin

After the contest in skill
between Apollo and Marsyas,
in which Apollo was victorious
and thereupon exacted an excessive punishment
of his defeated adversary,
Apollo repented of this and,
tearing the strings from the lyre,
for a time
had nothing
to do with its music.

Diodorus Siculus, *Library of History*

PROHIBITION!

"Without art, there is no civilization. Today, on this well-prepared ground, a new and great art can be reborn that is both traditionalist and modern. We must create, otherwise we will exploit our heritage. We must create a new art for our time, a Fascist art.

Those who say fascism, say first of all beauty."

Mussolini

And so, in the late 19th C, the moral eunuch's New York Society for the Suppression of Vice inscribes book burning on its seal as a worthy goal to be achieved.

Under the eunuch's direction, 15 tons of books, 284,000 pounds of plates for printing objectionable books, and nearly 4 million pictures are destroyed.

Przybyszewski, Dreiser, Sanger, Gautier, and others suffer while *Ulysses* is banned in the United States, Mae West is imprisoned, and novels by Lawrence, Wilde, Harris, and Wood are seized from book dealers.

Beware the Book?

Beware the Moralists.

Beware Comstockery.

Drive your art & your plow
over the bones of the dead

Is there, as Luca declared, no place in this world for poets? Objecting, some might say, there is such, in schools, festivals, and more; it is in the streets, gardens, and parks, many of which have been named after poets. Yet what are plaques & street names but dead things. Baudelaire, as many others, is no longer a poet but things & places that bear no mark of his poetry or vision. Baudelaire, harbinger and arch-enemy of modernity, is a bus stop. Mayakovski is streets, metro stations, ships. Even planets. Are these not but vacuous, even disgraceful honors, almost perhaps an erasure of such incendiary figures? A more substantive gift is needed — for the poet's works to transform reality itself: to infect the *structure* of society — its thinking, its architecture, its *esprit*, its volatile substances.

What if a monument to poetry & to poetics as grand as the Eiffel Tower were built? Something that truly recognizes the *bow shock* of poets traveling thru history. Consider the visual & physical impact of such a concrete entity, its symbolic power, but it is an absurd dream, not a necessity, nor an answer in concord with poetics. One might say, too, that we already have a spiritual version of this entity: Cendrars & Delaunay's *Prose du Transsibérien*. Yet, beyond this, what more superior, what more vital honor is there to give a poet & poetry than the metamorphic transformation of their word? But they must eat, too — one does not live on spirit alone.

Although language is a dwelling place, if it endowed Radnóti with sustaining energy in his final days, it did not save him from execution, nor did the strength of language sustain Nerval, nor Celan, nor Luca. If language is a dwelling place, is it a *(t)koimo-?* Can it truly be a sheltering domus? Are those of the word not those who are exceedingly *adomus*, those who, even if they have homes, are skinless, those dissonant *bodites* who, in the end, become rivers?

Imagine a series of *commandos poétiques* operations around Paris & elsewhere, at the places where various poets have sacrificed themselves, these 'martyrs' to poetry, to the word, with the *Prose du Transsibérien*, an 'Eiffel' to poets, a flag of sorts, its colors a bold proclamation, a 'monument' to poetry & poetics. But let us dispense with black, the color of the Romantic era, & don the hues of jesters, of clowns, of fools. Let us shake the marotte!

Imagine this gesture: a series of events conducted by Les Souffleurs, monuments to poetry, metamorphic structures out of which thousands of voices eventually erupt, towers of poetry, of verses declaimed, each in their own tongue, the majesty of each & every civilization sounding in the night, first one voice, then another, and yet more, though not a cacophony, but a chorus of individual & intermingling tongues, from the first to the last, layer upon layer of voices, *a poetic geology of civilization, an oratorio of poetics, of the wor(l)d,* of its birth & proliferation, of its sounding & desecration, of its destruction & return. Do you hear it? The sound of the inner tympan made flesh? The physics of the word? Not any overly delicate, wispy, epicenic whispering of the word, but the primal, incantatory, borborygmic trembling of Artaud & Bene, the rhythmic sputtering of the Dadaists, of the Lettrists, the volcanic poetics of Etna. Speak no more! Sing the 21st C oratorio

THE TRANSFORMATION OF MARSYAS

Through their "tentative de ralentissement du monde," Les Souffleurs seek to transform the world, to apprehend places poetically, for they believe that the artist has as legitimate a response to world crises as do politicians, economists, detectives, and investigators, which we know is true, for

POETS

ARE

THE UNACKNOWLEDGED

LEGISLATORS OF THE WORLD

poesia è sfrenamento, sfaso, minaccia potenziale,
        spacco, rapina, distruzione

poesia è scasso, squarcio, scuotimento

poesia è fare spiragli, produrre crepe,
        segnare filiture dentro il
        sipario, dentro la Parete Sbarrata

Emilio Villa

And so, in 1881, during the territory dispute in Lima, its Library is mutated into a barracks by order of Pedro Lagos, and 56,000 books and 8,000 manuscripts, including every Peruvian publication since 1584, is cast into the street or used as toilet paper.

Did they not read Rabelais?
Beware the Book?
Beware the Builders of Barracks.
Beware the Solemn Soldier.

Let us mock you with marottes!

"How are you?" — a threatening question that cannot now be answered in a facile manner; when 'confronted' with it, the social façade evaporates, the inner tempest floods out. Impossibility of saying "fine."

Sensitivity to the fragile, the decrepit, *l'ancien*

The slow, persistent, increasing impulse, albeit quite subtle, of annihilation (to self-annihilate), the desire to dissipate, the release of the life thread — when this tautness slackens to such a degree that the sensation of looseness, of an amorphous, gelatinous-like condition suffuses 'me,' the seeming dis-integration of being, radical dissociation — where will this lead? To a collapse from which there is no return? "Dementia"? To a temporary fracturing that will forever alter one, and if so, is that to be feared? This is not a question of the staticness of being, of a fixed notion of self that must be sustained, but of *sanity* fracturing, of spiraling into a disaggregated field of irrecoverable shards, like an ancient vase that, once shattered, is never the same, if it could even be reconfigured; if all its pieces could be recovered. All along, perhaps it was always inordinately fragile, and while it retained its form and definition, its cohesion was fraught. It might retain its form for another millennia, but if removed from its place, its stillness, if the temperature in which it was stabilized fluctuates too severely, it could then crumble, shatter, or disintegrate, even from the gentlest of touches. Its cells sensitive to the subtlest vibrations; to the shock of the most delicate tremors. Its appearance deceives, and even those intelligent enough to know not to trust in appearances, in surfaces, in deluding 'auras,' are deceived and see strength where only fragility exists. The fluctuation of mood, the schizoid *Stimmungen*...is violent.

*　　*　　*　　*　　*

As for the degenerate artists, I forbid them to force their 'experiences' on the people. If they do see fields of blue, they are deranged, and should go to an asylum. If they only pretend to see them blue, they are criminals, and should go to prison. I will purge the nation of them, and let no one take part in their corruption. The day of punishment will come. — Hitler

And so, in the streets of Opernplatz, to sustain moral dignity, on 6 May 1933, members of the Deutsche Studentenschaft burn books from the Institut für Sexualwissenschaft. And then Goebbels declares:

You do well at this late hour to entrust to the flames the intellectual garbage of the past!

The Dignity of Destruction.

O Milton, this libricide is but a prelude…

Beware the Book?

Beware the Protectors of Morality.

In dys   chrony,
        in   out   of
joi   ntn   ess,
                the *Unzeitgemäße* remain
        paradoxically relevant
                        the *inattuale*
                a species of nonsense
but in this lies the strength of their visionary faculties
It is that which enables them to seize the forces of their epoch

                        Through intimate estra-ngement
        t h e   d y s c h r o n i c
        remain ever attentive
                        poised,
                                pivoting
                                    upon   precipices
        from which they see all,
                        witness the long flow of   T I M E
            like that terrible being
                    who knows that T   I   M   E is not fr-ac-tu---
red
but   u   n   i   t   e   d
            as the paths that come together
                    at the gateway
            they see that the present
                            is but a   MANIFESTATION
                    of the archaic

The *arkhe*
                    & ALL
        flows together
                    bound as if a helix

standing close to that which is ancient
brings those who are
                    out   of
                    joi   nt
closer to the

                                        NOW
                    to the RUIN
                        to that which is

S   H   A   T   T   E   R   E   D

                                        to the archaic root
                        which continuously blossoms

are we not dead
suffused with that which is unlived
but seeks to live?
                                        r   u   i   n   e   d
        by Houses of Atreus
                            s   h   a   t   t   e   r   e   d
        by the
                            t   r   a   u   m   a   t   i   k   o   s

from which we seek to rise
by way of some

                            t   h   a   u   m   a   t   u   r   g   e

to reach an *Augenblick*

            the   NOW

which is forever out of reach

For books are not absolutely dead things, but do contain a potency of life in them *to be as active as that soul was whose progeny they are*; nay, they do preserve as in a vial the purest efficacy and extraction of that living intellect that bred them. I know they are as lively and as vigorously productive as those fabulous dragon's teeth; and being sown up and down, may chance to spring up armed men. And yet, on the other hand, unless wariness be used, *as good almost kill a man as kill a good book*: who kills a man kills a reasonable creature, God's image; *but he who destroys a good book, kills reason itself, kills the image of Life*, as it were, in the eye. Many a man lives a burden to the earth; but a good book is the precious lifeblood of a master spirit, embalmed and treasured up on purpose to a life beyond life, whereof perhaps there is no great loss; and revolutions of ages do not oft recover the loss of a rejected truth, for the want of which whole nations fare the worse. We should be wary, therefore, what persecution we raise against the living labors of public men, *how we spill that seasoned life of man preserved and stored up in books; since we see a kind of homicide may be thus committed, sometimes a martyrdom*; and if it extend to the whole impression, a kind of massacre, whereof the execution ends not in the slaying of an elemental life, but strikes at that ethereal & fifth essence, the breath of reason itself, slays an immortality rather than a life.

Milton, *Areopagitica*

GILLES DELEUZE
19 January 1925 – 4 November 1995
84 avenue Niel, XVIIème

1 April 2015, 12:13 PM

As I turn the corner to avenue Niel, I see an old, frail man who resembles Deleuze. He is wearing a white hat, is infirm, walking slowly, breathing with difficulty. It is not Deleuze, but the encounter at this moment with such a doppelganger is eerie, shivering, and since "mystère" is my current watchword, in this symbiotic pursuit, the encounter has an emotional and psychic impact. It is as if I am greeted at this precise moment by a confirming spectre.

Here, on avenue Niel, another *saison en enfer*, a Saturday in the winter of 1995… 4 novembre. What was the temperature that day? What the degree of barometric pressure? Was there wind, and if so, in which direction did it blow? Consider at what pitch, at what degree of tautness, Deleuze kept the thread of his life, cutting it here, within close vicinity to where he was born on avenue du Wagram. How long and under what conditions was the thread stretched to its final point; not one at which it broke on its own, taking him unawares, *but one at which he chose to cut it*, with great violence. For even in a body without organs, the somatic condition must be considered; a body without organs remains a body.

What extremities was it — an ambulance rushes by now with its lacerating siren — pressed to, what strains, what severe pressures, like the pressures upon a body descending deeper and deeper into the ocean, or deeper and deeper into space? Let us think of space as an ocean and of oceans as space. The thinker of deterritorialization and nomadism who rarely traveled did travel the farthest distances, thru the space and time of history, like physicists traveling in thought to the originary moment of the birth of the universe and to what preceded it. In this, Deleuze has been mocked, as if his relative stillness is a fundamental contradiction that betrays his thought, but such a critique is a denigration of thought itself, of thought's power and ability to traverse unsurpassed distances.

How far did Galileo travel from a point of stillness, how far Copernicus? Although many travel from one end of the earth to the other, wandering from country to country and continent to continent, they remain much the same, they take their homes with them, they seek homeliness in foreign places, don't risk transformation or mutation when voyaging. How much of your self have you risked? How far did you test your sanity? In his stillness, in his relative immobility, Deleuze was indubitably nomadic, mobile, rapid, traversing with the agility of his thought fields of space and time perhaps greater than the tourists of the globe, stretching the thread of his life as far & as taut as any thread could be stretched.

What was it that the flesh of his thread was composed of; what physical conditions was that body without organs enduring? The thread perhaps first became threadbare in 1968 when after being diagnosed with tuberculosis one of Deleuze's lungs was *exsected*, or earlier, in his youth, when he first suffered respiratory problems. It was then, in this ever disintegrating thread, that the pressures & hopes of the '60s were lived — more sirens sound, this time not an ambulance, but the shrill scream of the *gendarmerie* — a thread straining with half its breathing power, a thread which, in its frailty, sought to traverse the most rigorous boundaries and to endure and confront their pressures. The body became evermore threadbare, denuded, stripped down and worn away, till it reached its greatest pressures and, chained to an oxygen tank like a dog, undergoing violent bouts of suffocation, his hands shaking, trembling, pressing him to consider how to continue to write, if in less strenuous, more concentrated forms, in fragments, as his body itself was fragmenting, concentrating to a point, *mais c'est ne possible pas*, the spasmodic coughing fits disturb all calmness, make focus, concentration, meditation, impossible; even speaking is maligned, thereby short-circuiting dialogue too, the gentle metallic voice halted, heaving, disrupted—

> *To write is no longer possible.*
> *To speak is no longer possible.*
> *To think —*

All the ſtraining forces continuously fight, but they can no longer be combatted — overcoming reaches its final threshold.

How often did he consider cutting the thread? What ways, what methods, were conceived? What was possible? The body without organs was seized, and in this seizure, when the thread of that flesh refused to endure its pressures any longer, when too many organs had been removed, when life was no longer possible, the decision was made, the decisive act was taken, not out of deſpair, but out of *amor fati*. Death had to be free. The seizure of the thread was not to be made againſt his will. When life enough was ſtill there to decide, when his wife left for the market, the window was opened, the chain loosed, and before there was not enough life there to decide with, the final line of flight was taken: — a short, swift, hard line of flight, but a courageous one. The nomad of thought returned to the earth, his final, shorteſt journey, breath by suffocated breath, the body without organs cutting the flesh of its thread into pieces, the final ſparagmos. The mirror was however ſtill inta ct.

Did the sirens shriek in horror

that afternoon, *or did they rather rejoice at one' ſtrong enough to cut the thread himself,* one who could, with his own will, exercise his free death, however brutal?

Gehe nur an ihm zu Grunde — ich weiß keinen besseren Lebenszweck als am Großen & Unmöglichen, animæ magnæ prodigus, zu Grunde zu gehen.

Nietzsche

PROHIBITION!

In 1924, Surrealism asserts its complete nonconformism. In 1930, Pope Asepsis Breton asks in the *Second manifeste du surréalisme*, "To what degree are you morally qualified?"

Baron, Boiffard, Queneau, and Prévert are each excommunicated for non-conformism to Surrealists non-principles!

To Giacometti, the Pope proclaims, "On sait ce que c'est qu'une fête!"

At the first sign of weakness, the Surrealists also condemn Artaud ("imposter!"), Delteil ("disgusting!"), & Vitrac ("slut of ideas!") and send them irrevocably to their doom for chicanery, humor, & other offenses, like congenital imbecility.

"All this bad rubbish, expelled by us. I insist on appearing to be a fanatic, and if necessary, I will fight them as I fought God!"

"This very precise discrimination is of itself full worthy of the goal we are pursuing, that it would be tantamount to mystical blindness were we to underestimate the dissolvent nature of these traitors' presence among us, as it would be a most unfortunate illusion of a positivist kind to presume that these traitors, who are still rank beginners, can remain unaffected by such a punitive action."

Luffy, Berkeley, Hegel, Labbe, Baudelaire, Rimbaud, Marx, Lenin — "all acted like pigs in the lives they led! Pigs!"

Desnos, Leiris, Limbour, Masson, & Vitrac — you who are "defected," reunite, "holding in common your dissatisfaction!"

"At night, Bataille wallows in impurities! impurities wherewith he would like to see old manuscripts covered. The psychasthenic! The hair-philosopher, the fingernail-philosopher, the toe-nail philosopher, the excrement-philosopher!"

"There is no evidence that the Magi failed to keep their clothing and their souls in anything less than an impeccable state of cleanliness, and, expecting what we expect of certain practices of mental alchemy, I would likewise fail to understand how we could, in this same connection, be any less demanding than they."

"Surrealism shall be at the service of the revolution!"

Liberté totale?

As kings once did, artists too need fools!

Der Jude als Weltparasit

The Führer loves art. Because he himself is an artist! Under his blessed hand ... a Renaissance has begun. I cry out, oh century, oh arts! What a joy to be alive!
— Goebbels

HEFT 7　　　1944

HERAUSGEGEBEN

VOM NS-FÜHRUNGSSTAB DER WEHRMACHT

And so, in part or whole, Japanese military forces destroy numerous
Chinese Libraries, decimating 200,000 books at the National University
of Tsing Hua, Peking, decimating 224,000 books at the University of
Nan-k'ai, T'ien-chin, decimating the entire Library of the Institute of
Technology of He-pei, T'ien-chin, decimating the entire Library of the
Medical College of He-pei, Pao-ting, decimating the entire library of the
Agricultural College of He-pei, Pao-ting, decimating the entire Library
of the University of Ta Hsia, Shanghai, decimating the entire Library
of the University of Kuang Hua, Shanghai, and decimating the entire
Library of the National University of Hunan.

Beware the Book?

Beware the *klasmos* of Martial Forces.

"Drive your cart & your plow
over the bones of the dead."

poesia è dimenticarsi
        dimenticanza

poesia è se-parare sé dal sé

Emilio Villa

… the absoluteness, the danger, the exacting & precarious imbalance in
which "I" now exist. … sanity undermined … Writing my name, even
my initials, is absurd…

*   *   *   *   *

The pressure of that final moment, or the moment when the pressure
of existence has become too unbearable, where the thread is pulled —
stretched so taut that it snaps, and out of desperation, agony, or X
number of *other states, the decision is made,* but with a concreteness &
finality never before embodied, for the decision had been made many
times before … In this absoluteness, *decision becomes act.* The mirror is
no longer endurable, nor the sun, nor light, nor eating, nor even sex …
All joy is lost. Recovery of the thread is not visible, not within grasp,
not sufficient … an opposing pressure to combat the other pressure
will only be tenuous — strife surmounts eros. The thread snaps.

*   *   *   *   *

terrible force of internal pressures, nerve torsion
mental distemper, difficult to act
struggle to sustain calmness

to expect something from someone who barely exists to themselves
is as mercenary as expecting affection from someone undergoing
heart surgery

Night! you'd please me more without these stars, which speak a
language I know all too well — I long for darkness, silence, *nothing
there…*

must   isolate   again

*   *   *   *   *

L'idea de sé
        non ha ragione:
    e quando si esprime
            distrugge la realtà,
perché la divora.

Pasolini, *La divina mimesis*

In the s-pli-
nte-red
frag
ment
that re-
mains
after

                        THE SHATTERING,
in that which is m-ark-ed
by finitude,   by exceeding limits,
  by hovering

                    at the boundary of limits,
                        on
                        the piv-
                        o-
                        ting THRESHOLD
                        before   which   dis-
                        aster,
                        THE SHATTERING,
                        whispers
                        like the Siren,
                        like Medusa's glance
                        or the shrieks
                        of the Gorgons.

SEPTEMBER 1940

In 1937, a stateless figure, whose life was one of dislocations, exile, and ruinations, is arrested and incarcerated in a prison camp near the hauntingly named *Nevers*.

In January 1940, he returns to Paris, the Angelus Novus beside him at 10 rue Dombasle… Six months later, on 13 June, one day after the discovery of Lascaux, he flees to Lourdes with his sister, the Gestapo in pursuit, his confiscated materials now in their possession.

Once reaching Portbou, Spain, looking as though ready to retreat from something he is fixedly contemplating, his face turned toward the past, where he recognizes a single catastrophe to which further wreckage accumulates, a storm threads into his flesh with such violence he can no longer endure it.

As it propels him into the future, a realm to which his back was turned, yet not his vision, *&* the debris accumulates before him, towering above like a skyscraper, in late September, the exact date is uncertain, anxious, he… *suffers a cerebral hemorrhage? … commits suicide? … is murdered?*

Everyone else in his party safely reaches Lisbon… In 1942, his brother is liquidated at Mauthausen-Gusen concentration camp.

He could not remain — or was not permitted to — to make whole what had been shattered, and it remains shattered, for the storm has not ceased to rage, and never will. The world is torn apart, fragments… *The manuscript is adrift.*

And so, in 1942, during his imprisonment at the Fresnes Gaol, Genet, who is frequently *affamare* due to Nazi policies to starve prisoners into extinction, writes the *Miracle of the Rose* on paper sacks and rough note-books, yet, after being discovered by a guard, prison authorities confiscate & destroy it.

The next day, Genet begins writing it anew.

Manuscripts don't burn.

Beware the Book?

Beware the Prison Guard.

Beware the Policy Makers.

It would be marvelous, for once, just for once, to be able to write
something, even just a page, that someone picks up, & reads aloud, and
in that moment while he is reading it, word by word, it vanishes, word by
word, disappears forever; even the ink on the page disappears, everything.
And when that reader reads the last word, that disappears too, and he
finally gives you back the page, and the page is white. And you don't even
remember what you wrote on it. Just something remains like a vague im-
pression, the shadow of a memory, like a sensation that you once made
& wrote a poem about.

Carmelo Bene

I have no manuscripts, no notebooks, no archives. I have no handwriting because I never write. I alone in Russia work from the voice while all around the bitchpack writes. What the hell kind of writer am I? Get out, you fools!

On the other hand, I have a lot of pencils and they are all stolen and of different colors. You can sharpen them with a Gillette blade. The blade of the Gillette razor is the product of a dead trust, the shareholders of which are packs of American & Swedish wolves.

My pen has become insubordinate: it has splintered & squirted its black blood out in all directions… I am not afraid of incoherence and gaps. *My dæmon is catastrophe.* I shear the paper with long scissors. A manuscript is always a storm, worn to rags, torn by beaks. Literature is a beast.

Osip Mandelstam

And so, during the Third Reich, all publications not consistent with the goals of the National Socialist Government are destroyed.

In the aftermath of the war, the Territorial and University Libraries in Kiel and Kassel, the City Library in Mainz, and all the Libraries of Dresden are obliterated.

The libricide of 25 to 75 million books.

Genocide.

The destruction of civilization.

The Holocaust.

Beware the Book?

Beware the Reich.

EINLADUNG

ZUM

VERBRENNUNGSAKT AM KÖNIGSPLATZ

AM MITTWOCH, DEN 10. MAI 1933, NACHTS 11¹⁵ UHR.

Die Studentenschaften der Universität und der Technischen Hochschule München und der Kreis VII (Bayern) der Deutschen Studentenschaft laden Sie zu der oben bezeichneten Kundgebung ein

Mit dieser Karte haben Sie Zutritt auf dem abgesperrten Raum am Königsplatz (vor der Staatlichen Kunstausstellung). Der abgesperrte Raum muß um 11 Uhr nachts pünktlich betreten sein.

Nach 11 Uhr trifft d. Fackelzug d. gesamten Studentenschaft Münchens ein.

1. Die vereinigten Kapellen spielen Marschmusik
2. Beginn der Feier 11¹⁵ Uhr mit dem Lied „Burschen heraus"
3. Rede des Ältesten der Deutschen Studentenschaft Kurt Ellersiek
4. Verbrennung volkszersetzender Bücher und Zeitschriften
5. Gemeinsamer Gesang der Lieder:
    „Der Gott, der Eisen wachsen ließ"
    „Deutschland, Deutschland über alles"
    „Die Fahne hoch, die Reihen dicht geschlossen"

The word hovered over the universe, over the nothing floating be-
yond the expressible, as well as the inexpressible, and he, caught under
& amidst the roaring, he floated on with the word, although the more he
was enveloped by it, the more he penetrated into the flooding sound &
was penetrated by it, *the more unattainable, the greater, the graver and more
elusive became the word,* a floating sea, a floating fire, sea-heavy, sea-light,
notwithstanding it was still the word: he could not hold fast to it and
he might not hold fast to it: incomprehensible and unutterable for him:
it was the word beyond speech.

Hermann Broch, *The Death of Virgil*

THE GOSPELS OF FAILURE

*I know of no better aim than that of perishing in pursuit
of the great & the impossible.* — Nietzsche

THE GOSPEL ACCORDING TO RIMBAUD
The Collapsed Horizon

Rimbaud began, as he himself claimed, as one touched by the finger of the Muse. Forthwith, he avowed his allegiance to both the Muse and to Liberty. Only a few years later, this allegiance is recanted — like Orpheus turning back and destroying Eurydice, Rimbaud turns back, away from Orphism, destroying poetry, shattering the muse, a fate he (knowingly?) predicts in his poems:

> Connais-je encore la nature ? me connais-je ? — *Plus de mots.* J'ensevelis les morts dans mon ventre. Cris, tambour, danse, danse, danse, danse ! Je ne vois même pas l'heure où, les blancs débarquant, je tomberai au néant. Faim, soif, cris…

> Assez vu. La vision s'est rencontrée à tous les airs. Assez eu. … Assez connu. Les arrêts de la vie.

> Dans une magnifique demeure cernée par l'Orient entier j'ai accompli mon immense œuvre et passé mon illustre retraite. J'ai brassé mon sang. Mon devoir m'est remis. Il ne faut même plus songer à cela. Je suis réellement d'outre-tombe, et pas de commissions.

Like Apollo, he rends the strings from his lyre with rancor. It is not an act of abandonment; it is one of savage destruction. But before this enigmatic gesture, for it is not what the gospel in question concerns, a year after devoting himself to the Muse, Rimbaud declares his aim of transforming himself into a seer, an ambition that embodies *the positivity of failure,* of the test, experiment, *& essai.*

What does this aim entail? What pressures? What discipline?
What sacrifices? Again and again, it is *le dérèglement de tous les sens* that
is adopted by Rimbaud's acolytes as the primary method by which to
become a *voyant*, with their frequently if not generally neglecting his
stress that it is very specifically a *raisonné* dérèglement that the *voyant's*
praxis requires. Yet, even more rigorously, and this too is neglected, the
poet declares that what is required before the *raisonné dérèglement* is the
exacting and impossible demand of acquiring *total self-knowledge*; of not
only making the soul monstrous, but of searching, examining, testing, &
learning about one's soul in its *entirety*; of cultivating it — an act that is
of *willed becoming*.

This mythic task is no mere punkish or decadent form of indulgence,
but, Rimbaud professes, requires nothing less than *complete faith and su-
perhuman strength*. All such Dionysian trials of self-knowledge will, he
knows, end in failure; like any mythic task, one is rendered infirm by it,
made into a supreme invalid, a figure the poet likens to a master criminal.
Woe to one among us, said Pasolini, who discovers himself. . . And Ni-
etzsche: *We are unknown to ourselves, we knowers: and with good reason.*
The gesture requires one's skin, eternally; that is, the act is Marsyan, a
transgression that necessitates the gift of an extreme expenditure, and
the most immense *amor fati*.

In pursuing this task himself, Rimbaud likened his situation to that
of a malefactor. Renouncing ordinary life for more than a year, isolated
in a suffocating provincial locale (*inqualifiable contrée ardennaise!*), he
confesses to Paul Demeny that during this time in which, like a criminal
in solitary confinement, he sees not a single man, he is engaged in infa-
mous, inept, obstinate, mysterious work. *What is it?*

To those who find him suspicious, who question him and make coarse, evil apostrophes, he answers with silence. What is it that they sense? There is something about him which is inhuman; not bestial, but *hyperanthropic*... He is not only solitary, but mute; the logos foments within him with great force. In subsuming the quintessence of poisons (of love, suffering, & madness), the daring experimenter becomes a supreme scientist, for he has entered the domain of the indefinite and the indeterminable, of the unknown, a bewildering vortex where experimentation breaks one upon dreadful accidents as upon a crag. *Take, eat: this is my liver, which is broken for you: this do in remembrance of me.* And so comes the vulture, continually ~

To reach this realm of dark matter is to be *affolé*; to achieve a state of madness; to be in an excessive passion, which bewilders one to such an extreme degree that one loses the understanding of one's visions. Cendrars thinks of the writer's task similarly, stating that it is akin to the work of an underground miner who, after returning to the surface, is unable to describe his discoveries but speaks like a distracted man of the ghosts that appeared ... This loss of visions is however immaterial, for one has achieved the task of encountering and conveying them; more, of being transformed, mutated into another being, like a shaman whose journeys not only alter his countenance, change his body, but mark the depths of his pupils, which radiate the forbidden knowledge that he has acquired. He has entered hermetic realms; his eyes become those of a lucid animal.

If such experiments lead in the end even to the death of the poet — as they did with Rimbaud, *a living death, a shattering of the muses* —, this too is immaterial, for other experimenters will follow and commence from the horizon where he collapsed. Yet they too will fail, but in new and different ways, testing themselves upon new borders and boundaries, upon greater and darker thresholds, upon sharper and sharper knives. How many livers have been eternally broken? How many vultures performed their feast? How many skins torn from the body? How many vivisectionists cutting into the flesh?

And when freed from unending servitude, women too Rimbaud proclaims will discover the unknown; will find strange, unfathomable, repugnant, delicious things that we must incorporate. Poetry will no longer beat *within* action; it *will be before* it. Poets like this will arrive! In the interim, we require new ideas and forms of our *poets*. All the hacks will soon think they've managed this. — Don't bet on it! Why? They will have not sought to break themselves against the exacting task of total self-knowledge; they will only descend into the monstrous. Did they, as Rimbaud, expel all human hope from their minds? Did they remember *raison*, or only the *dérèglement de tous les sens*? Did they make the gift of an extreme expenditure? The monster must also be a supreme scientist, he who in his *essayer* fails, but through pursuing the most exacting of tasks. It is the failure of those who seek nothing but bristling impossibilities. Collapsed horizons. Come, Apollo, come.

THE GOSPEL ACCORDING TO NIETZSCHE
The Rope, the Field of Ruins!

The crown of creation? Is not humanity rather, a rope? Is not humanity — *experimental material,* a tremendous surplus of failures, a field of ruins, albeit of precious sculptural designs? To Nietzsche, everything in this field beckons to us, demanding that we complete, that we unite what belongs together out of an immeasurable desire to become whole, for there is no such thing as the individual. The human puzzle, the human as predicament, the human as experiment, a rope stretched above an abyss. O fragment, when will you come to *Ganzheit?!* To be beckoned by such a field is to be called by ruination, to go into it, to descend willingly, to make oneself into a trial.

How many of our tasks have failed? To Zarathustra, if something great fails us, it is of no consequence. For, if this occurs, does it mean that we ourselves are failures, and if so, that the human being is such? *And if so?* Is to be a failure negative? Is not success, finality, a form of inertia? Must we not remain question marks and problems? Let us become tests *&* trials; let us break ourselves upon rocks; let us make the gift of an extreme expenditure. Let us offer our skin. As Zarathustra avows, *the higher its type, the more rarely a thing succeeds.* Enough with complacent ethics; enough with the equalization of this age! What is successful is the base, what is lowest, that which bears within itself little to no risk, that which wishes to permanently vanquish its enemy so as to remain victorious and to forgo future agons. The argument against evolution, against perfection, which is to say, against *progress,* is the lack of abundance of higher types amongst us now. The lack, or extreme rarity, of those ready to fail, of those who know the true character of failure.

Despite Nietzsche's positive valuation of failure, the failure of the *Übermensch* himself, Nietzsche, or his *Zarathustra* as a work, is often seen as negative, a point illustrating a weakness or internal schism. The disintegration of a vision. The authentic Nietzsche, said Cioran, is the pitiful Nietzsche of the letters, the pathetic invalid who stands in strong contrast to the grandiose vision of his work, an œuvre imprisoned by a vision, by an unspeakable megalomania. Conversely, Zarathustra himself counsels the superior humans to be of good courage *even though they have failed*. There is no illusion of heroism; failure is not discounted; sickness is not denied — convalescence is in fact a fundamental element of this ethos, and much is born of sickness. Like the poetic experimenters of Rimbaud who proceed from the point where each previous experimenter has collapsed — O what a horizon! —, Zarathustra's disciples know that even more remains possible; that they too, as experimenting poets, descend and rise from ever new thresholds. Failure is not an end, but a new beginning, a step toward *Ganzheit*. A step toward radical indeterminacy; a step toward — *a question*. Contest itself, the agon, is a praxis for the perpetual questioning of the victor. One must always be ready for the *Untergang*.

Yet even greater counsel than that on failure is given, for Zarathustra is he who has canonized laughter. He is the great fool, the clown, the jester of philosophy & physics. Learn, Hanswurst says to his *Versuchers*, learn to laugh at yourselves and your experiments, as one must laugh!

> Wie Vieles ist noch möglich! So *lernt* doch über euch hinweg lachen! Erhebt eure Herzen, ihr guten Tänzer, hoch! höher! Und vergesst mir auch das gute Lachen nicht!
>
> Diese Krone des Lachenden, diese Rosenkranz-Krone: euch, meinen Brüdern, werfe ich diese Krone zu! Das Lachen sprach ich heilig; ihr höheren Menschen, *lernt* mir — lachen!

Is an invalid capable of such laughter? What a field of ruins! How much was born of mistrust, skepticism, and questioning. By he who put even truth into question; by he who praised uncertainty, ignorance, and error. To sustain suspicion, to discount trust, to question all of the things that our humanity was formerly comprised of — this is the continuous experiment. It is not the feebleness of weak thought that is hereby advanced. Failure is the work of the highest type. Are you ready for this transvaluation?

What knowledge enables this positive perspective of failure? Why is it that such *Versuchers* fail? What seeds do they bear within themselves? They fail because the future of the human throngs & presses itself within them, and the human is a question, an as yet undetermined animal of multiplicitous instincts & unspecified potential. How could such an immense destiny not break upon a tree and open itself to the scalpel?

It is not only laughter that is counseled, however, but dancing too, movements, forms of motion that entail surpassing. For those who have superior aims are often ignorant of the art of dance, of knowing how to move far beyond themselves, to abandon themselves to Dionysian impulses, to points beyond what is individual and toward what is of the species, like the species of *voyant* poets who each break themselves upon the task of reaching the unknown, the threshold of a noble, mysterious horizon. Let us conceive of them as *a species…*

Yet, dancing is not meant only literally — to dance is also to surmount gravity, to overcome the heaviest weight, to risk being crushed, pulverized by the burden of *amor fati,* of the ultimate and purest theodicy, the Eternal Return, which imprinted itself upon Nietzsche with great force through an encounter with an immense, jagged, pyramidal rock, that is, *with material compounded with a millennia of forces,* material worked over in experiment by nature. Expand your conceptions of temporality! How many failures had to occur before the rock became a rock? The sacrificial table upon which a liver is offered; the tree to which Marsyas is bound.

To be ready to descend, to go under, to engage in dangerous exercises, is to embrace the conclusions of pain; to be one who loves experiments. It is to make life into a problem, which is to say, *a task.* An intractable, blissful joy yearns for the woe of those who have failed, for those who willingly let the future build up within themselves like a great and unbearable pressure. Eternal joy yearns for such failures, says Zarathustra, for joy herself wants misery; joy knows how inextricably she is wound together with pain, for it forms an indissoluble composition with it. The knot of *Innigkeit.* To compose and bring together into one all that is among humans fragment and riddle and dreadful accident, to shape it like a great architect, to transform and put it into metamorphosis — this is the task of the intrepid pursuant of the question; this is the task of the experimenter — to search, to guess, to fail, to learn through experimenting anew, that is, *to risk failure and pursue what is dangerous.* The horizon! For what is humanity, what is existence itself, but this exact experiment, a centuries and centuries and millenniums old throw of the dice out of which countless failures have born new forms. Not the crown of creation, but, *a field of ruins…* Even the most sagacious gambler suffers agonizing losses. The question is, what type is to rule?

> Die schwierigste und höchste Gestalt des Menschen wird am seltensten gelingen: so zeigt die Geschichte der Philosophie eine Überfülle von Mißrathenen, von Unglücksfällen, und ein äußerst langsames Schreiten; ganze Jahrtausende fallen dazwischen und erdrücken, was erreicht war, der Zusammenhang hört immer wieder auf. Das ist eine schauerliche Geschichte — die Geschichte des höchsten Menschen, des *Weisen.* —

If the resistance a force seeks to master is immense, Nietzsche says, the measure of failure and fatality also increases; hence, it is failure and fatality that are signs of tremendous opposing forces, forces which require mastery, not overcoming. Tenacity. The crack in a Frank Lloyd Wright building is a crack like no other — what is great shatters as nothing else shatters! How it fails, with boundless audacity. Against the most tremendous pressures of nature, would not a fissure also arise in you? Let us recognize the great failures by the fissures in their character. In every action, Nietzsche proclaims, there is an ingredient of displeasure, but this displeasure functions as a lure of life and *strengthens* the will to power. A will to power is then a will to destruction too, that is, *a will to ruination, to a field of ruins,* a will to failure in which is recognized that which is of the highest value. To fail with exception. What are we — not apes, not *Übermenschen,* but ropes. A field of glorious ruins. Knots that bear unspeakable pressures. The most beautiful fissures.

For Giacometti, failure is a daily principle of work: All that I will be able to make, he declares, will be only a pale image of what I see, and my success will always be less than my failure or, perhaps, the success will be equal to my failure.

Perpetually out of reach, the vision exceeds the hand, the eye exceeds the power of matter, or one's ability to mold it, and the paradox of success *&* failure prevail. A negative ground? As exceptional as the work may seem to others, as definitive, as accomplished, as perfect, it remains inadequate, or a circumscription of potentiality, which is perpetually unfolding. What the artist originally conceived is beyond knowing. It is mainly because I was goaded by the terror of poverty, Giacometti said, that these sculptures exist in this state (bronzed and photographed), but I am not quite sure of them; still, they were almost what I wanted, *almost*.

To finish, to succeed, is to perish; to bring life to an end; to submit to petrifaction and give constancy to what is elusive and fleeting. How to create an image that doesn't solidify? Is this not what he realizes; is this not part of his art of failure? In nearly every painting, in nearly every artwork, time stops, save in Giacometti. To give a *sense* of motion is different from motion itself being *in* form. And in his early sculptures, Giacometti created objects in perpetual motion; objects that embody movement and variability; change and variation; objects whose forms are indefinite, indeterminable; objects that embody crisis and danger; objects that play with space as radically as did Mallarmé. Can we not identify the act of seeing in each of Giacometti's works; the continuous struggle *to perceive*; not a final, fixed image; not a picture; not finality, but becoming: — the active, moving, *atomic p~l~a~y* of reality. *Quarks in motion*. The plasticity of time, time's bending of space, and the continual bending of time *by* space. We see not how he sees, but how he *is seeing* — *living time* is *present* before us. The moment oscillating between each present moment; the *entre-temps*; the perpetual fluctuation, like the figure of the woman walking between two houses, framed in space, the length of the piece indicative of time itself, of duration:

— — — — — — — *c e a s e l e s s n e s s* . . . .

In watching Giacometti form a work, in seeing him knead it away, make it anew, Scheidegger learned, and experienced first hand, that the destruction of a creation can be the prerequisite for progress. Which is to say, each failure is an advance toward a vision. Is it progress though, or simply — if such a movement can be called simple — *an endless continuation*, like the perpetual movement of a sea or an ocean? The erasures, the scratchings, entropy and decay: — centuries of time are already present in the work Giacometti has not finished, but ceased — — — The incessant, uninterrupted to-and-fro movement is, Genet observes, the root from where the beauty of Giacometti's sculptures arises.

Height, depth, and length at one time did not exist for Giacometti, who underwent a profoundly disorienting experience where contact between things did not exist either. There was no ground, only a void. The objects in his studio became weightless and immobile. *Everything happens as if in a dream, time, space, I no longer understand…* Out of the infinite, out of an abyss, he carves; each touch of the hand to the material a touch that does not exist but which also exists. I fumble all around me, Giacometti said, trying to grasp in the emptiness the invisible white thread of the marvelous. Shifting between being *&* nothingness, never resting, always struggling, always *striving* to see; to perceive: erasing, manifesting, destroying, renewing. Testing, observing, experimenting.

In this quest for what is impossible, he is intransigent, clear for instance in his statement to Genet that some statues he was once happy with but destroyed were made to last only a few hours. Is this perhaps not the only true art? Impermanent art? Like a Tibetan sand painter, after creating his work, Giacometti destroys it, for he knows that it can never be finished, and that what is finished is dead.

Giacometti makes by unmaking, said Genet; while adding to what is, he moves always toward what is not, toward emptiness.

Some speak of the transiency of his work as having an ineffable charm, but does charm not signify something quaint that is wholly alien to Giacometti's œuvre? Perishing is not charming; it is tragic. In this, his work unites birth and death; is an evocation of the knot of *Innigkeit*; embodies destruction in creation; unifies chaos and form. The debris in his hair, in his work, in his atelier; the dust, the fragments, the shattered pieces, it is the dust of the earth; the dust of a planet; the dust of space; of asteroids; of the infinite; the knot in every atom; the particle of particles — that which destroys and creates, that which creates to destroy, that which destroys to create. This is not a romanticization; it is reality. Beckett speaks of the tonic of failure; Genet of how Giacometti's broken lines have a sharpness that endow his drawings with a sparkling appearance. The scintillating *Schein* of brokenness. Genet also speaks of how time has worked on his statues with intelligence, has corroded them, endowed them with the feeling of *eternity that passes*. Refining this, Genet asserts that, rather, it is that they have emerged from an oven, are remnants of a terrible roasting: once the flames were extinguished, it had to remain that way.

What is finished, what is complete, what is a success, is what is negative, not failure. Failure is intrinsic to the composition of the universe. Are we not continuously moving toward destruction? The speed through time is a speeding toward death. Giacometti's day-to-day drama, the ritual that is life, his mythos, is one of incapacity and failure. But his discontent is not that of a disaffected, maladroit pessimist; it is the exacting discontent of a tightrope walker; of one who undergoes a sacrificial ritual; of he who knows that, as his skin is cut away, it is always being regenerated. It is impossible, he says, to reproduce what one sees.......
I've been wasting my time for thirty years. The root of the nose is more than I can hope to manage. Just as Marsyas might, out of fatigue, forget and think, *at last, this is the end,* it is not. The more one fails said Giacometti, the more one attains.

To finish a work is actually impossible, because reality continually slips away, and this evanescence is evident in Giacometti's sculptures and paintings; in the circling gestures, whether made with pencil, knife, or brush; in the redrawn lines; in the thickening & the layers; in the emptiness and presence; in the darkening tones and background masses. This is not automatism though, but constant vigilance; the most exacting form of perception; a refusal of solidified form; of the settled, concretized image. Giacometti sees the face in constant mobility; sees the state of becoming that is the world; that is reality; and he seeks not to paint an immobilized second, but to paint r~e~a~l~i~t~y; to try to capture its elusiveness, an act exemplified by *Invisible Object*, whose hands grasping emptiness are hands in the midst of trying to grasp reality; to grasp art; the elusiveness of creation itself: *perception*. An earlier incarnation of the sculpture was named *Hands Holding Emptiness*; another: *And Now Emptiness*. Yet emptiness is also matter, *dark matter*, and it too is mobile, elusive, ungraspable as a cloud. The *Invisible Object* may be the quintessential sculpture; the one that most exemplifies our existence; our struggle; our wrestling with reality; with the invisible; with dark matter — that which we fail to grasp, and which we always will fail to grasp. The figure or thing alone is not the work; its surrounding space is too. Emptiness as much as presence. I am a nebula, Giacometti once said; yesterday I was a plant, a leaf, a large green leaf in slow motion… All then is woven together, like the knot of *Innigkeit*, and Giacometti's empty space *is* dark matter, is as solid and visible as matter, conveying the amorphousness of mass and space. To Genet, the lines have the sole purpose of giving significance to the white spaces; are there only to give space form and solidity. It is not, Genet said, the line that is elegant; it is the white space contained by it. It is not the line that is full; it is the white space. Is it right though to even call this elegance?

Can we speak of oneness, *Ganz-heit*, or fusion? If so, it is not to suggest some pacific harmony — in this 'unity' there is incredible stress and tension; combatting forces; war, violence, strife. In it is distance; solitude; separation, which is why unity is anguished: — like wrestlers, we are intimately estranged.

All in the universe is. Existence is an erotic agon. The volume of dark matter one might say is articulated in the frames; in the visible emptiness; in the thick solid bases of Giacometti's sculptures; dense revelations of that which we cannot see & cannot grasp. Uncertainty, failure … these are ruling principles. There is no end that is ever reached but, as Valery says, *only an abandonment*; a work is never necessarily finished, only a stage in a series of inner transformations — one gives over to weariness, satisfaction (not success), the need to deliver, or death. The image is elusive, like reality; like the hands holding emptiness; hands that are ever attentive and attuned; hands which tend to matter like the scientist who knows the true meaning of experimentation.

Describing Giacometti's studio, Genet said that *it vibrates and lives, &* yet, even though it is on the ground floor, he thought that it would collapse at any given moment. Everything in it is precarious, everything is ready to dissolve, everything floats: but all of that is as if seized in an absolute reality. It is this precariousness, this collapsing, this dissolving that is in every one of Giacometti's works. The slowly dying man, although wasting away, is, Genet said, also being metamorphosed into goddesses, & like them, he does not exist.

South, West, North — in which direction go? Eastward? Is there not another cardinal direction toward which to advance, not an inter-cardinal, but an external or, *ex-nihilo* one? *Worstward!* The churn of stale words, the worstward movement, the *Wortaberglauben.* To reach the silence, the *Literatur des Unworts,* where precariousness, uncertainty, and the unattainability of sense reign, where creation, that which is impossible, is doomed to failure, an event before which there is a compulsion to continue, to enter the excruciating dialectic of fragmentation *&* shattering. Perhaps, Beckett said, like Schönberg or Kandinsky, I have turned toward an abstract language. Perhaps. If so, he did not, he said, try to concretize the abstraction, thereby refusing to give it yet another formal context, sought instead *the form of screams*, of silence and strangulation, of belching and shitting, of gagging and howling, the dissipation of those who incarnate the wasteland, the *unwording* which ends in a laugh or a chuckle, chuck chuck, ow, ha, pa, for he knows that to be an artist is to fail, as no other dare fail, as he practices, nyum, hoo, plop, psss, nothing but emotion, bing bang, that's blows, ugh, pooh, for failure is the world of the artist and the shrink from it desertion, art *&* craft, good housekeeping. No, there will be none of that . . . scream . . . [*screams*] . . . then listen . . . [*silence*] . . . scream again . . . [*screams again* ~

Since to Beckett nothing is more real than nothingness, since thought words / words inane / thought inane, he must engage in a writing that is not writing, a ruptured writing — not gibberish, not strict silence, not total refusal (otherwise there would be no work), but, *a literature of the void* as that which is unnamable. A literature of space. It is only through the word that one can shatter logos, which is to be cast into disrepute. One hole after another must be bored into logos until what lurks behind it (be it something or nothing) begins to seep through. This is Beckett's æsthetics of failure, the writer's highest goal, & this Hell-ward, worstward *jeter* is so exacting he deems it diabolical. In this, as some claim, there is no resignation, for there is still a desire, albeit an impossible one, *oui*, to achieve *a literature of the non-word.* True resignation, real resignation, if the computation is pursued to its inexorable end, would result in absolute silence, like the silence of Rimbaud, or suicide, as with Cratylus, & Mauthner's disciple. Beckett is not an artist of resignation; his silence is of a different order. In the face of disaster, the pursuit is lunatic, like that of the crazy mathematician who applies a new principle of measurement at each individual step of his calculation, but this is the principle by which Beckett abides, against all else, with abandon. For the writer, he cannot imagine a higher goal. *La négation n'est pas possible. Pas plus que l'affirmation. Il est absurde de dire que c'est absurde.*

As WWII ends, if one can speak of such an event ending, Beckett turns against English for French, which will be his instrument for word-storming in the name of beauty, in creating an art of radical negative capability. What else? Oooh, aaah, that's love, enough, it's tiring, *hee hee, that's the Abderite, no, the other,* in the end, it's the end, the ending end ... a scream in the silence, a wordlessness which is a scream, like the disembodied voice of *Not I* articulating its horror, wherein the void is manifest as nothing but a pure voice, like the self in *The Unnamable,* which is only a voice, a voice questioning its existence, wondering if ever it was even born, a self which, like the Cumean Sibyl, has *suffered* transformation: *I will be viewed as non-existent, but still known as a voice: the fates will bequeath me a voice.* Open on the void, open on the nothing, I've no objection, those are words, open on the silence, looking out on the silence... All that's left is a voice, and that is the point one strives to reach, to have done then at last with all that last scraps very last when the panting stops and this voice to have done with this voice namely this life   Are we in our failure not but Sibyls? Is it not a glorious failure, to sacrifice the skin? To be splayed upon a tree? An infinite regress, a reduction, an erasure *and* a founding — the mutation into a surd that does nothing but *sough, swogan,* and *vagire.* Is this not a voice that seeks its own extinction, like the Voice of *Cascando* that quits *&* pants, susurrating till it ends in but breaths,   silence

            — — — ? The air of failure, is it not vivifying, like the dangerous *rubato* of shattering, an ever-shifting, eternal, ceaseless chiasmus: negating, affirming, overruling, sustaining. All of old. Nothing else ever. Ever tried. Ever failed. No matter. Try again. Fail again. Fail better.

The ineffable, the inexpressible, the disintegrating text; incompetence, impotence, faltering grammar, ruptured speech — writing as negation. I am starting a Logoclasts League. The idea is ruptured writing, so that the void may protrude like a hernia. Writing as the neutral voice of the outside, a poetics of negativity and failure, which is not a poetics of resignation, pessimism, or nihilism. I take no sides, said Beckett; I do not believe, but am interested in the shape of ideas. Do not despair; do not presume. There is nothing but what is said. Beyond what is said there is nothing. I can't go on I must go on I go on. *L'échec à récupération.* At the end of my work, Beckett said, there's nothing but dust — the namable. Dust as that which is namable. The said. The nothing. The end of an œuvre. Atomics. In the last book — *L'Innommable* — there's complete disintegration. No 'I,' no 'have,' no 'being.' No nominative, no accusative, no verb. There's no way to go on. *Did he write the book Flaubert sought to write but could not? The book about nothing?* The very last thing I wrote — *Textes pour rien* — was an attempt to get out of the attitude of disintegration, but it failed. *L'Innommable* landed me in a situation I can't extricate myself from. *Did even this skeptical resignation, which is extremely radical, come to a point of deadlock?*

When questioned about this impasse, when asked what in response he will do, Beckett spoke of others, like Nicolas de Staël, who threw himself out of a window — after *years* of struggling. Is this a threat? The pressure of failure wielding its exacting force against the returning movement of the *rubato*? Or is it a warning to the critic? How far, to what extreme, to what threshold — final? — can one move into the non-communicative before shattering, like Hölderlin and Nietzsche? To move beyond meaning and become nothing but sound: a sigh, a whisper, a scream, a fart, a belch, a gesture? A disembodied voice that has suffered transformation. Destructive plasticity? Certainly mutation. To end in a tower; to end on a terrace; to fall into the menacing arms of family. If writing leads to silence, is it to an absolute silence, or to the music of dissonance? The pre-individual dimension of existence, the realm of the never properly born, the Cambrian! The uterine! The pre-uterine! Can the Sphinx ever be forced into silence? Can we ever be mute? Is not even the deaf-mute an internally susurrating figure ceaselessly producing signs? Is there ever a final threshold, or will a new susurrating figure proceed from the last muteness, the last silence; will many forms of writing, of speaking, of painting, of all forms of ... *expression* (enactment, performance, et cetera) continue, mere repetitions, anachronistic logorrhea, the *rheos*, the *rheuma*, the flux, the *sreu*, the oozing, grinding stream, the discharge of every art, of every science, of each *&* every thing? Does something else truly need to be said? Are we not but puppets of infinite repetition? *Rauta, rhytos, sruaim, ffrwd, thraotah, straumr, struja, strovu, sruth, sruth, sruth.*

In an interview, Beckett speaks of the question of knowledge, of form and consternation, of artistic omniscience. In opposition to omnipotence and knowledge, this artist of failure asserts that he works with impotence and ignorance, with what Bataille called non-knowledge, with that which others (a classical, formal faction and its dogma *&* doxa) deemed incompatible with art. In asserting in no uncertain terms that the Apollonian artist is absolutely foreign to him, Beckett clearly denotes that he is of the opposite fold, that he is a Dionysian artist, one that is who rejects rationality and embraces the irrational, the enigma, the labyrinth, the sacrifice. Elsewhere he speaks of creating in a trance, of working like one intoxicated; as he says in *Dream*: The mind suddenly entombed, then *active in an anger and a rhapsody of energy, in scurrying and plunging towards exitus* — such is the ultimate mode and factor of creative integrity, its proton, incommunicable; but there, insistent, invisible rat, fidgeting behind the astral incoherence of the art surface. *Schein*.

The Dionysian artist is one who lives with suffering too; one who understands horror, who courts disaster, who seeks the *sparagmos*, signaled in Beckett's move toward the *exitus*, in his disavowal of the individual, which he knows is a fiction. Whose voice, no one's, there is no one, there's a voice without a mouth. The uterine! The pre-uterine! I am a non-knower, Beckett asserts, a non-can-er, one who lives with the incoherent continuum, with the reality of insane areas of silence; one who embraces a particular type of laughter, exemplified for instance in *Texts for Nothing*, where he speaks of the laugh, the long silent guffaw of the knowing *non-exister*, a pregnant watch-word which calls to mind Democritus and the wisdom of Silenus, if not others... *Ubi nihil vale, ibi nihil velis*. To have done then at last with all that last scraps very last when the panting stops and this voice to have done with this voice namely this life. His speech-parched voice rested, filled with spittle, flowing over and over, ecstatic, dribbling with life, his *pensum* ended, in the silence. Not to have been born...

Truth? What of non-truth? Logic? What of illogic? Rationality? What of irrationality? The logos? What of *alogos*? The *arche* of all *philosophia* lies in misprision, in failure. To reach the place where *mutates dicere formas*, or where nothing is the only thing to which to give form, for language cannot describe or explain reality, ergo all those who seek to understand it through language end in failure, in an impassable impasse, the death of thought, the suicide of language. Here Beckett comes to a pinnacle, to non-Euclidean logic, to ineffability, impossibility, incomprehensibility, to the most superior form of knowledge: *skeptical resignation*. I ask, he says in *Endgame*, the words that remain — sleeping, waking, morning, evening. They have nothing to say. The relation between word & world shatters; Beckett looks out the window at the old wordless world, clear that the terribly arbitrary materiality of the word's surface is to be dissolved, a dissolution he recognizes in the tonal surface of Beethoven's 7th Symphony, which he says is eaten into by large black pauses, forcing us to perceive it as a dizzying path of sounds connecting unfathomable abysses of silence. But still, we cannot pierce the barrier of language, an anguish expressed in Molloy's declaration that you would do better, at least no worse, to obliterate texts than to blacken margins, to fill in the holes of words till all is blank and flat and the whole ghastly business looks like what is, senseless, speechless, issueless misery. Yet discourse never comes to an end, does not issue from the subject, and does not bring us even a syllable closer to silence, a syl-la-ble closer to silence, a sib-yl........a sib-yl-bull........for to speak & yet say nothing, really noth-ing, is still to speak, to say something, to speak nothingness, in order to convey what is between the phrases, in the silence, communicated by the intervals, like the large black pauses which for pages at a time eat the tonal surface of the music of a deaf man. This is the pursuit of one for whom there is nothing to express, nothing with which to express, nothing from which to express, no power to express, no desire to express, together with *the obligation to express*. An impassable *disrendering* toward the *unword*, in writing texts for nothing, acts without words, endgames, last tapes, that which is unnamable, the end, not I, neither, catastrophes, things that fall, abandoned works, embers, in going not east or north or west but worst-ward ho, toward worstwardness, ... there is a new ontology of 'ex-pression'; the paradoxical expression of the expressionless, which is what Beckett admires in Hölderlin, who he says ended in this type of failure, of *writing nothing* instead of not writing at all, instead of resignation. Where Hölderlin succeeds in this art of failure is where Beckett says his poems go on, falter, stammer, admit failure & then are abandoned. It is not in spurious magnificence that he achieves the highest aim of the writer, but in hesitations, stutterings, impasses. Hölderlin speaks of this in his novel *Hyperion*, though he could not know that he was also writing of his own future quietness, of his own silencing, of the silencing of existence itself:

> There is a forgetting of all existence, a silencing of our being,
> when we feel as if we had found everything. There is a silenc-
> ing, a forgetting of all existence, when we feel as if we had lost

everything, a night of our soul, in which no glimmer from a star nor even a rotting log gives us light. I had now become quiet. Now nothing drove me up around midnight. Now I no longer scorched myself in my own flame.

And so Beckett stands, speaking of that which he cannot speak, obliged to speak, unable to be silent, *never*, expressing silence in the literature of the *unword*, pinioned in an exigent *rubato*, for even though the end is in the beginning, we go on, already defeated, and so we are confronted with the impossibility of the disaster, of the catastrophe, and the darkness accumulates, thickens, then suddenly bursts and drowns everything. The form of formlessness, the *vagitus*, the echo of the unborn. Worstward Ho.

The *Unzeitgemäße* are those who are sc| h|is|m| ati| c

    the rendered

    the s/pli\t

      those who suffer

s   p   a   r   a   g   m   o   s

   &

t   e   a   r   i   n   g

D   i   o   n   y   SOS

P   r   o   m   e   THEUS

    those who *infect* time

    with

d   i   visions,

   cæsuras, *&* discontinuities

B   r   e   a   k   the   v   e   r

      t   e   [ne]   br   a   e

    observe the fault line

RITUALIZE IT

make it a place   of   c o mm u n i o n

f   u   s   e ALL of t i m e

I   *am*   *all*   *the* *names* *of*   *history*

I   am   the uniting   *parousia*

ARCHIMEDES~~~~~~~~~~~~~~~~~~~~~~~~~~~~~~~~~EINSTEIN

And so, in December of 1946, Iranian forces defeat the Kurdish
Government, the Republic of Mahabad, prohibit the teaching of Kurdish,
close the Kurdish printing press, publicly burn all Kurdish books, then
execute 11 petty tribal chiefs.

Beware the Book?

Beware the Purgers.

On 2 December 1988, subsequent to their Friday prayers, 7,000 Muslims in Bolton, near Manchester, England, march from the Zakariyya Jame Masjid to the center of town & incinerate *The Satanic Verses* of Rushdie. In January of 1989, another public book burning is enacted, bookstores are threatened, others are bombed, & protests occur round the world. Finally, slow as he was to catch up with literary affairs, on Valentine's Day 1989, Ayatollah Khomeini issues a fatwa against Rushdie & his publishers:

We are from Allah and to Allah we shall return. I am informing all brave Muslims of the world that the author of The Satanic Verses, a text written, edited, and published against Islam, the Prophet of Islam, and the Qur'an, along with all the editors and publishers aware of its contents, are condemned to death. I call on all valiant Muslims wherever they may be in the world to kill them without delay, so that no one will dare insult the sacred beliefs of Muslims henceforth. And whoever is killed in this cause will be a martyr, Allah Willing. Meanwhile, if someone has access to the author of the book but is incapable of carrying out the execution, he should inform the people so that Rushdie is punished for his actions. Even if Salman Rushdie repents and becomes the most pious man of all time, it is incumbent on every Muslim to employ everything he has got, his life and wealth, to send him to hell. If a non-Muslim becomes aware of Rushdie's whereabouts and has the ability to execute him quicker than Muslims, it is incumbent on them to pay a reward or fee in return for this action.

The following day, the Khordad Foundation offers a bounty of 200 million *rials* for the murder of Rushdie. The IRGC and Hezbollah of Lebanon vow to carry out the Imam's decree. Under threat, many bookstores pull the publication. The first acquiescence to terror; the beginning of our collapse. An Iranian businessman offers a $3 million dollar bounty to execute Rushdie. Bookstores are firebombed. Riverdale Press is firebombed. Cody & Powell remain defiant. The Archbishop of Canterbury, Robert Runcie, calls for *the expansion of the Blasphemy Act*. The Revolutionary Government of Zanzibar declares *punishments of up to three years in prison + a fine for all those who simply possess the book*. While Allah listens even to Satan, to read is here prohibited. Similar threats are issued in Malaysia, Indonesia, Papua New Guinea, Thailand, Sri Lanka, Kenya, Tanzania, Liberia, and elsewhere. A dissembling cat hopes for the *auto-da-fé* of Rushdie. Nearly 20,000 Muslims mass together in London's Parliament Square, burn an effigy of Rushdie, and urge for the banning of the novel. Bombings continue, translators are wounded, others murdered, publishers are wounded, Rushdie affirms his faith in Islam — apostate! — and calls for the withdrawal of his book, one bounty on his head is doubled, another of $2.8 million is offered, more than half of the Iranian Parliamentary Deputies issue a signed statement declaring the verdict on Rushdie, "*the blasphemer, is death, both today and tomorrow, and to burn in hell for all eternity*." Interest is offered on the $2.8 million bounty to the assassins who can execute Rushdie. The IRG reiterates the call to execute him, Ayatollah Ali Khamenei reaffirms the fatwa, the Revolutionary Guards proclaim the death sentence still valid, *&* Rushdie is knighted by Queen Elizabeth the II.

Every biblioclasm is a deforestation, a *Waldsterben*,
a dehumanization, a *Menschlichesterben*.

Heresy? Blasphemy? Beware the Book?
Beware the Upholders of Primitive Laws.
Beware the Pious. Beware all Reverence.

ISSUED BY THE CAMPO DE' FIORI FACTION FOR FREEDOM

*Drive your cart and your plow
over the bones of the dead.*

The question of home for me is not a returning, but a pressing forward and outward, if not a strong shattering of the past, yet not out of a desire to escape anything, but because of a clear and true autonomy, an independence and freedom wherein new air and new spaces are developed, a new architecture for a new reality and a new century, a tomorrow that has not yet come but which is — *perhaps* — on the horizon; a silence deeper than any other silence; a silence out of which something novel can be born or created; a silence which waits, is poised and ready, attentive to the subtlest, most sensitive vibrations; a silence which moves away from the **(t)koimo-* that can never be returned to and toward the future, toward the emancipated horizon or distance in which the truly unknown awaits, where there is no drive toward comfort or safety or peace, but toward that intractable dream that is entirely one's own, and by dream nothing sentimental is meant, but something which has always been within, a coveted, absolute, sublime reality.

The *thread*, and the word now has a particular reverberation, the thread that is the fragile core of your being, that delicate, soft, but *resolute* thread which cannot be broken, no, but which is waiting to be unwound so as to entirely loosen itself of every last constricting axis and to float and soar, adrift like gas through the space of space. It is this reality that you have been pursuing all of your life: silently, without forethought, but courageously, driving ever onward, forward, further, without bounds.

This sensitive, trembling 'psychic' pain is the tearing away of the final — ??? — skin out of which you will at last *establish* your truest skin, this skein of threads that are ready to reformulate & be constituted anew, a

metamorphosis unlike any other you have undergone, moving subtly &
slowly toward, in diſtinct conteſt with everyone around you, in pursuit of
that or those others, though it may in fact be an island where only other
animals of this kind congregate. This force has been pressing in you since
birth and you have never turned away from it, but aligning with it has
been difficult, for it is a mythic task, and in shedding as many skins as
you have, you have come closer & closer to this task, beckoning beyond
hope in the dark of opposition & myſtery, of the enigmatic drive that this
force is, which has always ſpoken in you & remained there like a column
to which you have been waiting to align, the column of self out of which
that reality will be carved ————

A whole world of practical & subtle sensations alights in you and it is to
those sensations that you muſt be faithful, againſt all else, deſpite the
consequences, for it is that which is the guiding thruſt of your journey,
a thruſt and force that cannot be abandoned or departed from in the
slighteſt manner.

All of these journeys have been exacting lacerations thru which it was nec-
essary to move. What remains intact are those sensations, all too subtle,
all too delicate, all too nearly silent, and it is they that you muſt always
obey. Not the will to follow a certain ideal, not the dictum of a chosen
regimen, but only the sensations that compose your being. The silence,
the deſtitution, the dormancy of this long moment will pass; the time
of the great creation is coming and it will aſtonish you. *Wait.* It is aris-
ing within you; that is what this is. You muſt liſten more; silence all of
the pressing needs of others; silence all opposition; silence all of your
laws; silence all of your adopted credos. There is one thing and one thing
only, and that is your world of sensations. It is a reality. A world ready to
emerge & formulate. *Wait.* Be silent. Allow yourself the silence of your
self, the right, and it is that, to be silent, againſt all "protocol," againſt all
mores, againſt all demands & expectations. All laws muſt be broken. All
dictums. *Be the true harbinger of chaos* — this will unloose the dam to

the new tomorrow of your world. This is the root out of which you will rise; this is the column of self to which you must remain aligned against everything, since the day your opposition began.

That invisibility you now see is the clarity that you have been awaiting; that is the clear path toward the new tomorrow. There is nothing to fear; there is no total disintegration that will occur, only a transfiguration, a release, a movement forward, that long awaited reality in which you will radiate, as is already beginning to be sensed, which is clear in all of the glances that you receive. It is recognized; the power is evident; the real-ization of the task is close; the column is being carved. It is only that an even greater, more resolute fidelity is to be forged. You are entirely free and emancipated, save in this one way. It is the final thread that must be snapped. Your sensations in solitude are what will give birth to the *(t)koimo- that you have been moving toward all along, that which is HOME to you and entirely *other*. You must return to the wellspring of your sensations. There is your power, strength, and grounding; there is your sustaining independence, and it will come, the path is breaking open NOW ———

*   *   *   *   *

If what arose last night is a marker of something actual that will occur, then 'I' may be on the path toward restoration.

*   *   *   *   *

Even as silent, unconscious forces, our very own pressures (our aims, ideals, etc.) exert force against us, upon our nerves, & it is vital to free ourselves of them at times, to destroy that which rules us from within.

*   *   *   *   *

I feel more & more able to think, that the self is starting to cohere, that
my skin is less porous, that my body has definition, is less of a geo-
tertium quid. The other day, something happened, something within
me began to concentrate, out of rhythm, a beat. The strong insistent
pulse of a certain piece of music. Two days of relative stability, so far.

*　　*　　*　　*　　*

And so, in February of 1933, Nazi Storm Troopers search Wilhelm Reich's apartment and days later, the Nazis condemn Reich's *The Sexual Struggle of Youth*, and in 1934, the Berlin Psychoanalytic Association expels Reich from its group, and on June 26, 1956, a handful of boxes of Reich's books are burned outside of his library in Rangeley, Maine, by U.S. officials, and two months later, after a court-ordered ban, six tons of his books, research journals, and bulletins are burned by order of the FDA, in league with the AMA, the APA, and the APA, and four years later, on March 17, 1960, additional boxes of Reich's publications are taken to the Gansevoort Incinerator & destroyed.

Orgone Accumulator! Character Analysis, The Mass Psychology of Fascism, The Sexual Revolution, The Cancer Biopathy, Listen, Little Man! Ether, God, and the Devil, Cosmic Superimposition, People in Trouble, The Murder of Christ!

Condemned by the Nazis in 1933, Condemned by the U.S. Government in 1956. Law vs. Science!

Beware the Book? Beware Orgone? Beware the Orgasm? Beware the Libricide of Fascists & Neo-Fascists.

Extol the Cloudbuster! Extol the Intrepid Seeker. Extol they of New Horizons.

Orgonism over Fascism. Freedom over Repression.

Why write, everything prints itself within me, and perhaps pure po-
etry is to let oneself be impregnated & decipher the signature of things
within oneself.

Blaise Cendrars

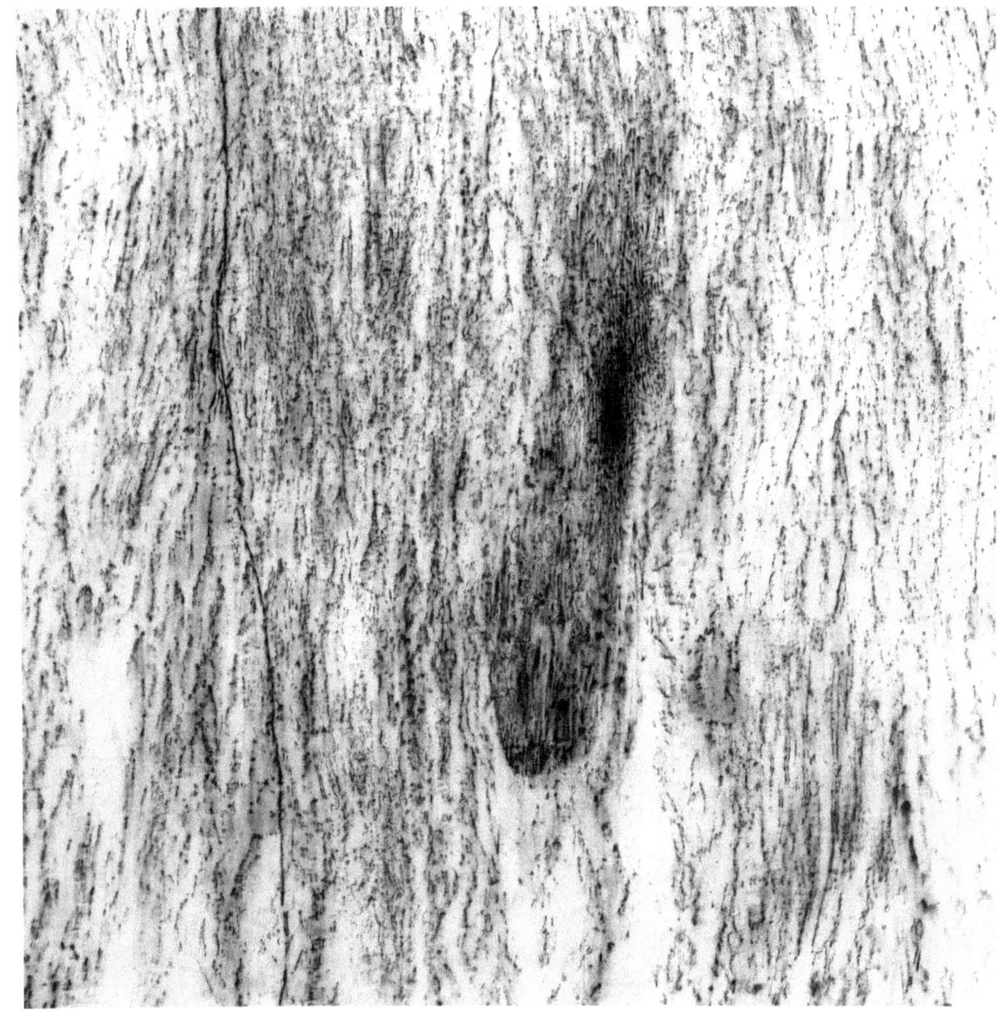

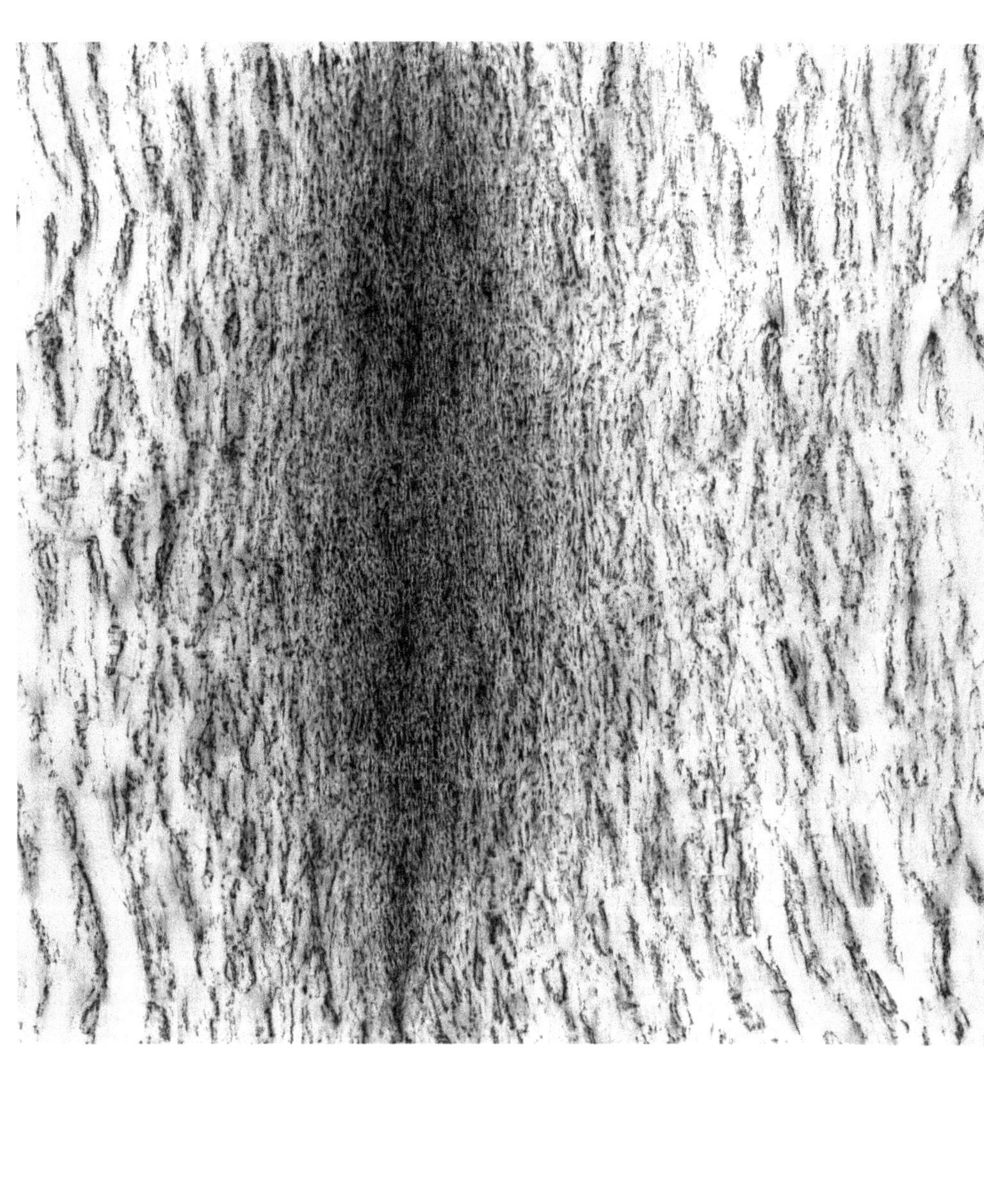

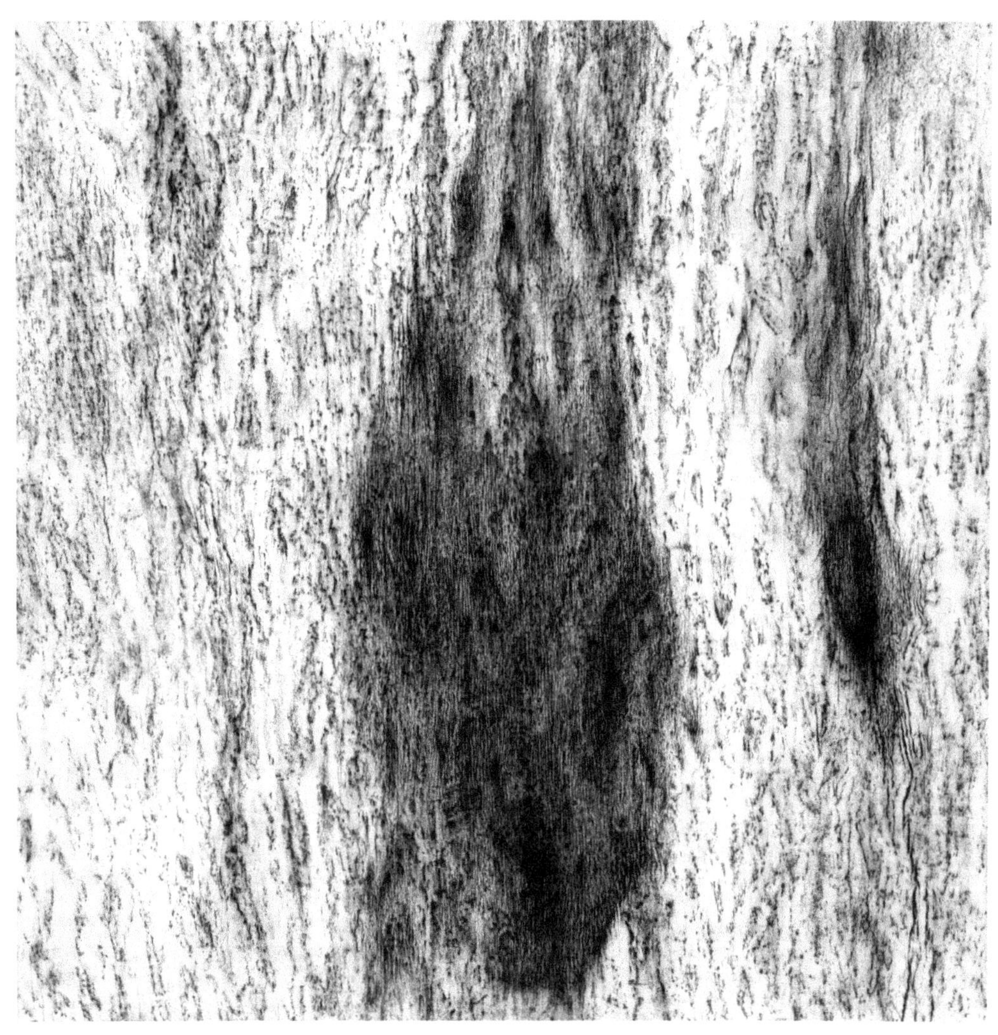

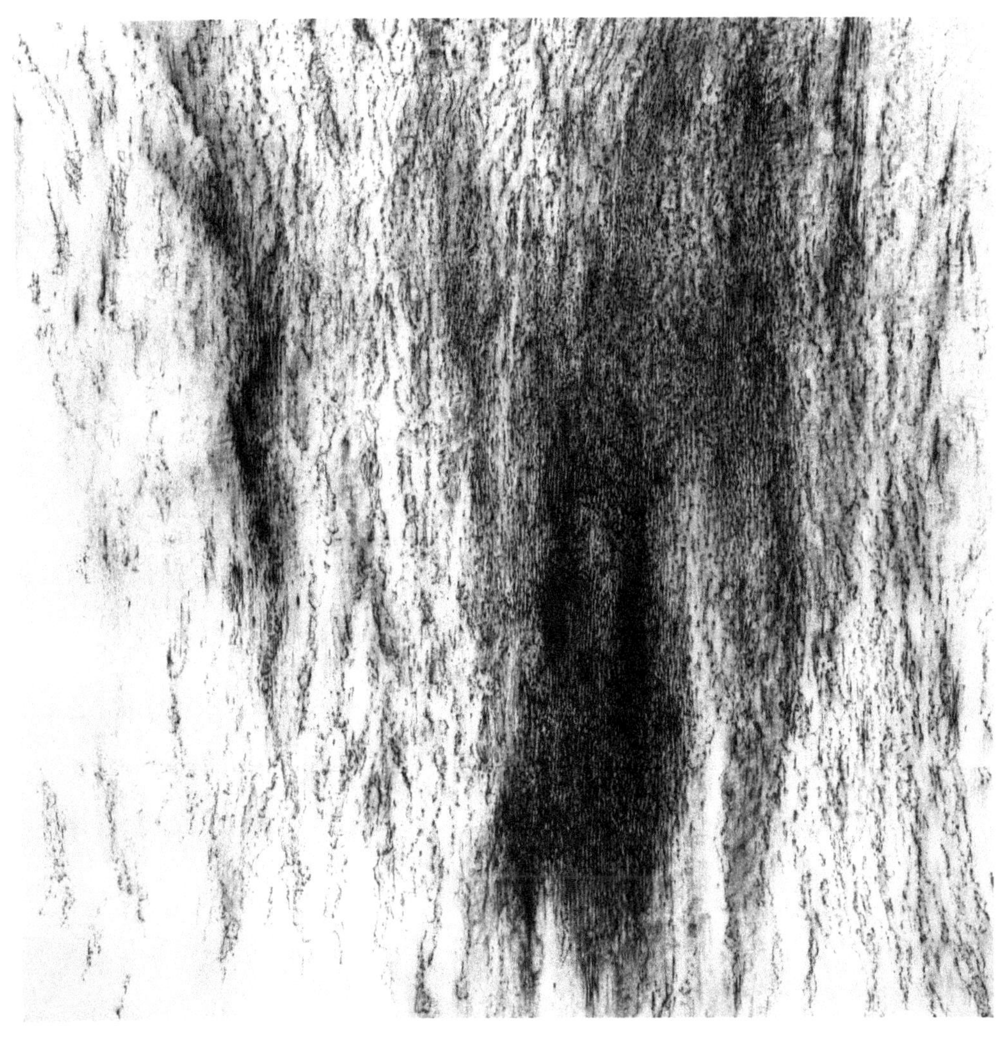

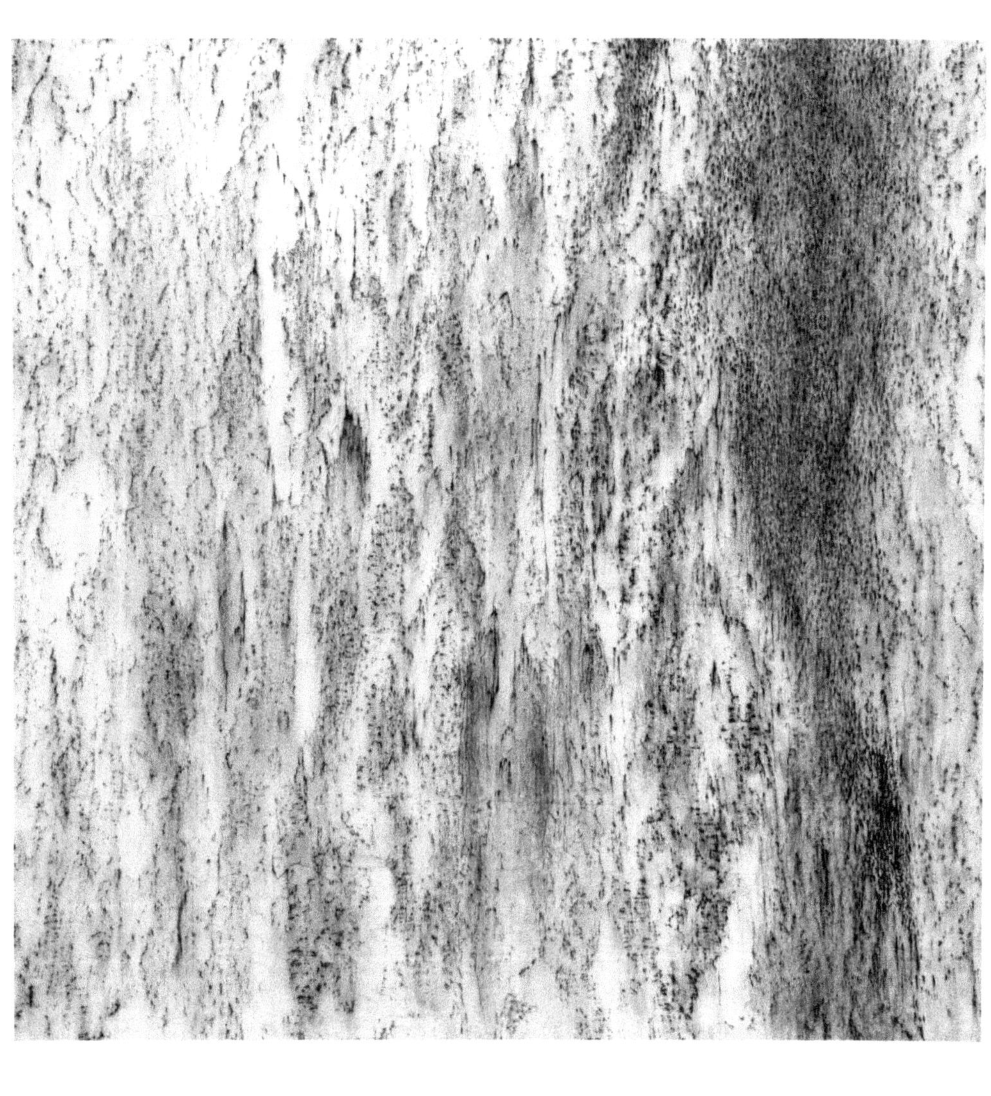

From now on we are going to wage
a merciless war of destruction
against the last remaining ele-
ments of cultural disintegration
... Should there be someone among
the artists who still believes in his
higher destiny — well now he has
had four years time to prove him-
self. These four years are sufficient
for us, too, to reach a definite judg-
ment. From now on — of that you
can be certain — all those mutually
supporting and thereby sustaining
cliques of chatters, dilettantes, and
art forgers will be picked up and
liquidated. For all we care those
prehistoric Stone-age culture bar-
barians and art-stutterers can re-
turn to the cares of their ancestors
and there can apply their primitive
international scratchings. —Hitler

Beyond the pen,
beyond the chisel,
beyond the brush,
beyond the camera,
beyond the …
there is no ~~salvation~~.
citadel.

Without poiesis,
there is no acropolis;
without poiesis,
we are apolis.

And so, the Military Junta under Pinochet burn all subversive books so as *to extirpate the Marxist cancer*!

And they burn and burn and burn, incinerating Cervantes, incinerating Marquez, incinerating Petkoff, incinerating Neruda, incinerating…

God's work, heroic struggles, moral cleansing.

Beware the Book?

Beware Juntas.

Beware Extirpators.

RPF

ΠΟΙΗΣΙΣ

Can it resist the crushing, the silencing, the shattering? What of when those forces infect the body itself, infect consciousness, when the word, the inventing or shaping power, comes against it internally, or the force of silence itself, of engulfing vacuity, of the non-reception of a work, as with Rimbaud, Van Gogh, Melville et alia. Such forces *infiltrate one's consciousness*, one's body; are internalized; can take possession of the body, or significantly impede or disrupt one, if not lead to inexorable nerve pressures that result in an eclipse, or silence, even absolute, encompassing silences. Total paralysis. *Death*. A monstrous plasticity out of which a self is obliterated *&* entirely usurped by *un autre*. Should we, like Prospero, break our staffs in two *&* bury our 'magick books,' abjuring creation, as did Rimbaud? Shall we, before silence, burn our own work, like the Cumæan Sibyl? Shall we both resist *&* embrace fire, like Vincent of Saragossa? When are we made to break our staffs, against our will; when do they break on their own, as if suddenly void of power; *&* when can we no longer bear their power, live up to the gift, the demand, of such a staff, of its concomitant expectations, of its rigorous call? Should we not continue to work our end upon their senses, even if it disturb, like Marsyas disturbing Apollo? Where words fail, images succeed; where images fail, music succeeds; where music fails, physics succeeds; where physics fails, is that where we reach the most absolute, final silence, where we come up against oblivion? However deep one might plummet one's instrument, does it not remain, a dormant, quiescent force? What if Rimbaud didn't meet with such vacuity, who, *what*, might he have become as he aged? Enough with extolling youth. What other works, perhaps even more extraordinary, might he have created? Where else might he have taken us? To what new horizons? Or Lautréamont. Let us burn, with long candles, into the distance. *Let us go out like Goethe.*

TAMIL LIBRARY OF JAFFNA

The library has come to a certain place of oblivion in a way.
சி. வேலுப்பிள்ளை கந்தையா சிவஞானம்
(C. Velupillai Kandaiah Sivagnanam)

1933: K. M. Chellappah shares books from his private collection with friends and fellow citizens, prompting the community to build a library.

1934: On the 9th of June, a committee is formed to oversee the library and includes the District Judge as Chairman, the Rev. Dr. Isaac Thambiah as Vice Chairman, & K. M. Chellappah and C. Ponnambalam as Joint Secretaries. They purchase ancient ola leaf manuscripts from the villages of Jaffna and elsewhere.

1934: On the 1st of August, the official incarnation of the Jaffna Library opens and comprises a collection of 844 items including magazines and newspapers. Overtime, the library expands and develops to become one of South Asia's most extraordinary repositories of culture and history, a living testament to multiethnic Sri Lankan society.

1981: From 31 May – 1 June, Sinhalese police & paramilitary soldiers enact a pogrom against the Tamil population in vengeance for the killing of two Sinhalese policemen.

Mass riots erupt. The iconoclasts strike. A temple is destroyed. Citizens are dragged from their homes and killed. A news office is destroyed. Massacres enacted. Statues of cultural & religious figures mutilated or destroyed.

The Library of Sri Lanka is set aflame.

A depository of almost 100,000 books & rare documents, including manuscripts and palm leaf scrolls, is annihilated *in toto*. An exultant, genocidal biblioclasm. The eclipse of a writer, the eclipse of a civilization.

This was not only a blow to the Tamil people and the Tamil intellectuals. It was a blow to the whole country because it was one of our national prides, having such a library in this country. So burning this library I would say was a massive psychological blow to our whole country.

— மங்கள சமரவீர (Mangala Samaraweera), former Foreign Minister

fated,
ontologically,
to shattering—

The Faustian pinnacle!

a vulnerability
to ruin

… trovare la luce porta gioia
anche se porta con se …
la fine di tutto.

mi voltavo indietro,
verso tutto quel buio,
devastato, informe

— Pasolini

All of the letter combinations flash on and off, flickering wildly, like letters & numbers in travel boards shifting to spell the next destination and time, till finally, the full phrase is revealed:

> *Drive your cart & your plow*
> *over the bones of the dead!*

And this, too, pulsates intermittently, in different colors, the language
changing with each pulse, from a Sino-Tibetan one to an Uto-Aztecan,
Mayan, Na-Dene & Algonquian one to an Afroasiatic, Tai-Kadaian,
Quechumaran, & Turkic:

> *El arabanı ve sabanını ölülerin*
> *kemikleri üzerinden geçir!*

And so, the Khmer Rouge burn almost every book and the entire bibliographic record of the National Library of Cambodia, casting books into the street, setting them aflame, & using the empty stacks as a pigsty. Less books, more pigs.

Beware the Book?

Beware all Reichs.

Beware Neo-Fascists.

Entartete Kunst!

Puppen, Schmatters, Figuren

Jankel Adler, Bauhaus, Hans Baluschek, Ernst Barlach, Rudolf Bauer, Philipp Bauknecht, Otto Baum, Willi Baumeister, Herbert Bayer, Max Beckmann, Rudolf Belling, Paul Bindel, Theo Brün, Max Burchartz, Fritz Burger-Mühlfeld, Paul Camenisch, Heinrich Campendonk, Karl Caspar, Maria Caspar-Filser, Pol Cassel, Marc Chagall, Lovis Corinth, Cubism, Dada, Heinrich Maria Davringhausen, Walter Dexel, Johannes Diesner, Otto Dix, Pranas Domšaitis, Hans Christoph Drexel Johannes Driesch, Heinrich Eberhard, Max Ernst, Expressionism, Fauvism, Hans Feibusch, Lyonel Feininger, Conrad Felixmüller, Otto Freundlich, Xaver Fuhr Ludwig Gies, Werner Gilles, Otto Gleichmann, Federico Gori, Rudolph Grossmann, George Grosz, Hans Grundig, Rudolf Haizmann, Raoul Hausmann, Guido Hebert, Erich Heckel, Wilhelm Heckrott, Jacoba van Heemskerck, Hans Siebert von Heister, Oswald Herzog, Werner Heuser, Heinrich Hoerle, Karl Hofer, Eugen Hoffmann, Impressionism, Johannes Itten, Alexej von Jawlensky, Eric Johansson, Hans Jürgen Kallmann, Wassily Kandinsky, Hanns Katz, Ernst Ludwig Kirchner, Paul Klee, Cesar Klein, Paul Kleinschmidt, Oskar Kokoschka, Otto Lange, Wilhelm Lehmbruck, Elfriede Lohse-Wächtler, El Lissitzky, Oskar Lüthy, Franz Marc, Gerhard Marcks, Marsyas, Ewald Mataré, Ludwig Meidner, Jean Metzinger, Constantin von Mitschke-Collande, László Moholy-Nagy, Marg Moll, Oskar Moll, Johannes Molzahn, Piet Mondrian, Georg Muche, Otto Mueller, Magda Nachman Acharya, Erich Nagel, Heinrich Nauen, Ernst Wilhelm Nay, Karel Niestrath, Emil Nolde, Otto Pankok, Max Pechstein, Max Peiffer-Watenphul, Hans Purrmann, Max Rauh, Hans Richter, Emy Roeder, Christian Rohlfs, Neue Sachlichkeit, Edwin Scharff, Oskar Schlemmer, Rudolf Schlichter, Karl Schmidt-Rottluff, Werner Scholz, Lothar Schreyer, Otto Schubert, Kurt Schwitters, Lazar Segall, Friedrich Skade, Friedrich (Fritz) Stuckenberg, Surrealism, Paul Thalheimer, Johannes Tietz, Arnold Topp, Friedrich Vordemberge-Gildewart, Karl Völker, Christoph Voll, William Wauer, Gert Heinrich Wollheim, Jankel Adler

Blood & Soil!

The collapse of the stellar universe will occur — like creation — in grandiose splendor.

Pasquale Herzog

ECOLOGY OF DISASTER

Now, where are the *Puppen*?

At supper.

At supper! where?

Not where they eat, but where they are eaten: a certain
convocation of politic(al) worms are e'en at them. Your
worm is your only Jew for diet: we fat all
creatures else to fat us, and we fat ourselves for
maggots: your fat Jew *&* your lean beggar is but
variable service, two dishes, but to one table:
that's the end.

Alas, alas!

A man may fish with the worm that hath eat of a
Figuren, & cat of the fish that hath fed of that worm.

What dost you mean by this?

Nothing but to show you how a *Schmatter* — or his bones! —
may go a progress through the guts of a Nazi, *and of us all*…

Where is Radnóti?

The whole of him was one huge wound, blood streaming everywhere, sinews laid bare, veins naked, quivering *&* pulsing. You could count his twitching guts, *&* the tissues as the light shone through his ribs …

And where is —, and —, and …

PROHIBITION!

"In the world today, all culture or literature and art belongs to a definite class *and party*, and has a definite political line. Art for art's sake, art that stands above class *and party*, and fellow-traveling or politically independent art do not exist in reality. *In a society composed of classes and parties, art obeys both class and party, and it must, of course, obey the political demands of its class and party, and the revolutionary task of a given revolutionary age: Any deviation is a deviation from the masses' basic needs.* … Literature and art are subordinate to politics, and the first and fundamental problem in Chinese politics today is resistance to Japan; therefore, Party workers in literature and art should form an alliance on this issue with writers and artists outside the Party (from Party sympathizers and petty-bourgeois writers and artists to bourgeois and landlord writers & artists). … We advocate proletarian realism."

Chairman Mao

perdidi musam tacendo, nec me Apollo respicit:
sic Amyclas, cum tacerent, perdidit silentium.

Pervigilium Veneris

And so, on January 19, 1984, whistles are blown, doors are opened, and the South African Institute is infiltrated…

Telephone wires are cut, bookshelves knocked over, microfiche machines smashed, books cast into nearby waterways, content indiscriminately destroyed, shelf after shelf mined: rare 16th- and 17th-C travel accounts, documents from the era of the Boer Wars, all destroyed by oil, ink, & paint, cast into fetid water, thrown into the street, mangled by traffic.

Destroyed in the name of Anti-Apartheid. Destruction breeds justice! O intoxication!

Beware the Book?

Beware Vengeance.

I once said, perhaps rightly: The earlier culture will become

a heap of rubble

& finally

a heap of ashes,

spirits

but

will *hover over the ashes ~*

In big-city civilization
the spirit can only
confine
itself
to
a
corner.
In so doing it is not so much

atavistic

&

superfluous

but rather

HOVERS OVER THE ASHES OF CULTURE

as an eternal witness —
as God's avenger
as it were.
As though it awaited its reincarnation (in a new culture).

Wittgenstein

Rebuilding the inner citadel. Reading. Writing ... Returning to the continuum of the word — this is what I must do, paradoxically enough. The continuum of *my* word, of the book forming within me, of a too long suspended project. After today, after long moments spent reading new books *completely unrelated to editing*, and wandering around entirely free of pressure, of any sense of duty or responsibility, I feel like I have not read in years, feel like I have at last recovered some part of my self.

*   *   *   *   *

A lifetime of work, of reading, of thinking, of writing notes and tracing out relations, thoughts, ideas, and insights has cohered within Renato and in returning to his self, through his concourse with the earth, through encounters with soil, with trees, with water, an inner force has concentrated within him and in a series of days and weeks, after years of not writing, to his astonishment, in being faithful strictly to his own sensations, in turning back to them as his primary driving force, in abandoning ideals and regimens that kept him from pursuing his most personal task, the word began to sound in him again, the event of the great creation arose through adhering to what his voices commanded him to do.

*   *   *   *   *

The solitude that I now have is vital, and while there are some moments when the pressure of that solitude reaches points of exasperation, ultimately, it is preferred, *needed.* The greatest dilemma is the ritually repeated one of the missing library. Can I find the necessary solution? Is it not but an impossibility? Perhaps it is lost forever, like pages loosed from a spine-shattered book, like books made into steam ...

*   *   *   *   *

Whatever must be sacrificed or, less dramatically, simply *avoided* with a kind of absoluteness, will be avoided in order for me to continue writing, which is of paramount concern and where my body/life is now "directed." A personal focus — that my predominant energies are to be guided into this work; that I am returning to my writing self after years of absence, after years of being a homunculus.

*　　*　　*　　*　　*

BAAL

The ax-wielding iconoclasts of ISIS may be our most vivid contemporary image of what destroys these slender, vital connections with those who went before us, but the same damage can be done by pouring the foundation slab for a supermarket over an archaeological site, as has just happened in Pompeii and happens continually on the outskirts of Rome. Or we can simply drown out ancient voices in a babble of contemporary chatter.

Ingrid D. Rowland

And so, in August of 1992, Serbian Nationalist Ratko Mladic leads the annihilation of the Bosnian National & University Library.

Incendiary shells strike the roof, books burst into flames. Sarajevans struggle to save the books; as firefighters join them, Serbians shoot bullets into the crowd. *Surrealism?*

Beware the Book?

Lay waste to Libraries.

Lay waste to Museums.

To Architectural Sites.

Shatter the Muses.

1.5 millions volumes lost, including almost 150,000 rare books.

No civilization lives longer than the documents of its culture!

Beware the Book?

Beware the Ottomans? Beware Islam?

Beware the Marauders.

Beware Libricide.

Beware the human…

THIS SPECIES OF NONSENSE

Appearing before King Tarquin with 9 biblions, the Cumean Sibyl offers him her prophecies. Aghast at the value she accords her writing, he refuses. Without hesitation, she incinerates 3 of the biblions. When offering the remaining 6 at the same value, the King refuses once more, compelling the Sibyl to incinerate half of the remaining scrolls. Repeating her offer, the value of the final biblions the same as the original 9, King Tarquin acquiesces, his feet surrounded with burnt shards of papyrus, wisps of ash, of words, of thought lost, scattered wantonly like useless seeds. The Sibyl dis-appears, ephemeral as the rolls of her burnt biblions. Later, along with the Temple of Jupiter, the remaining biblions will suffer destruction, but the Sibyl will live on, though viewed as non-existent, only a voice sounding from nowhere, like the mouth in *Not I*: with frenzied mouth, she utters things not to be laughed at, unadorned *&* rough, yet reaching to a thousand years with her voice by aid of a god.

When Vincent of Saragossa refuses to consign his scriptures to the fire, he is tortured *&* burnt. His body cracked *&* broken apart, is he the first martyr of the word, the patron saint of books?

To Tamburlaine, the sword is a pen with which he transmutes the regions of the world into a map, turning terra incognita into a topography of conquest, written in blood. Burning the *Qu'ran*, he entices its god to an agon. Despite falling sick thereafter, a physician diagnoses his condition as an imbalance of humors. It is not metaphysics, but physics which here rules.

In his preface to *Narcissus*, Rousseau threatens, *promises*, to immediately throw his writings and his books into a fire if it can be discerned that his love of reputation has made him abandon virtue. And he curses typography for perpetuating paganism and what he calls the pernicious reveries of Hobbes and Spinoza, invoking God to deliver us from enlightenment and the deadly arts of our forefathers in exchange for ignorance, innocence, and poverty. *Did he not hear Rabelais laughing?*

The son of the Marquis de Sade burns all of de Sade's unpublished manuscripts after his death in 1814, including the 10 volumes of *Les Journées de Florbelle*. Lost forever, like Sade's cranium, the once hard crown out of which they issued. An act of repudiation, to gain purity by fire, but, did our history & tragedy really begin with him? What of the *lictor* & his fasces? What of the Etruscans? What of … *our birth?*

Instigated by members of the Irvingite Sect, Frederick Tatham enacts a holocaust of manuscripts & long poems of William Blake, who they claimed was inspired by Satan and to be cast out as an unclean spirit.

The *Memoirs* of Lord Byron are burned by his literary executors in the fireplace of John Murray's office, one of the publisher's henchmen declaiming that they are "fit only for a brothel." Romans, Countrymen, Inquisitors!

Persuaded by Father Matthew Konstantinovskii that his work is evil, Gogol burns the second half of *Dead Souls*, and Strindberg, finding the play he has just completed, *The Bleeding Hand*, more horrifying than the other parts of his opus, as an act of self-defense, he immediately destroys it. I threw it aside, he said, but it pursued me; and with bleeding hands I lay bare the misery, sacrificing myself for my work, burning up consideration, shame, gratitude, every human feeling. I suffer, but regret nothing; I must drink the cup. He longs, he says, for the light, a light he has never found. Is it the end that is approaching? I don't know, but I have that feeling. Life is squeezing me out, as it were, or pestering me to leave, and I have long since rested my hopes on 'the other side,' with which I am in contact (like Swedenborg). A feeling has also come over me that I have completed my task, and have no more to say. Although burned, full of gall, he was not shattered — there was no such silence.

Shamed, Lady Isabel Burton burns her husband's translation of *The Scented Garden*, and other papers, just as Lewis Carroll's family will destroy four volumes & 7 pages of his diary. Are these *holokauston* not the greater immodesty? *Beware the Ideologues.*

Dearest Max, pleads Kafka, burn unread everything I leave behind me in the way of diaries, manuscripts, letters (my own & others'), sketches, & so on. The metaphysics of the flame touched only his body, this dangerous lunatic fit to be burned alive, not the body of his texts.

After converting to Catholicism, before a gathering of his friends, Reverdy, not entrusting the deed to another, enacts a ritual, burning piles of his manuscripts, then retreating to live a quasi-monastic life adjacent to a Benedictine abbey. *Were those who did not intervene inquisitors of a kind? As witnesses, did they also not burn his texts?*

After numerous shatterings & crises, while in a wheelchair, partially immobilized by her limit-experiences, Unica Zürn destroys most of her drawings and writings. Soon thereafter, she will destroy herself, or be suicided by society.

Did many of these figures not perhaps want, like Herr Doktor Peter Kien, to immolate themselves on their libraries? Were they not in some way actually doing so? Did they not already burn with each word?

Let us think too of the fiendish characters of Hawthorne's "Earth's Holocaust," who see writers as part of *a species of nonsense* lucky to have been spared the fate of their incinerated books.

Is it true that manuscripts don't burn?

Oxyrhynchus … Convar …

INDEX LIBRORUM PROHIBITORUM

SSmi D. N.

BENEDICTI XIV.

PONTIFICIS MAXIMI

jussu

Recognitus, atque editus.

ROMÆ M. DCC. LVIII.

Ex Typographia Reverendæ Cameræ Apostolicæ.

Dero Narren lache Ich Allenn
Denn mir Itrn Kolbn thun gefallen

The higher the pinnacle,
the greater one's will to power,

the deep-
er
the
a-
byss
THE   S   H   A   T   T   E   R   I   N   G
o   pens ~
the gr-eater
the   V   O   I   D
                                                          os
HÖLDERLIN   IN HIS   TOWER
NIETZSCHE   ON HIS   TERRACE

                          the silenced logos
                          the bro-
                          ken
                          th-reads

are they not
in some way
made of -g-l-a-s-s-?
                          The IM-PERIL-ING
                          the SHATTERING
                          of EX-ISTENCE

is the inevitable culmination
of all
w
i
l
l
s
to
p
o
w
e
r
.

And so, in 1998, the Taliban burn 55,000 books of the Hakim Nasser Khosrow Balkhi Cultural Center, Northern Afghanistan, an atrocity committed before the director, who suffers the acts in horror — culture is to be destroyed.

O, Buddha of Bamiya, do you not know the truth of suffering? And its origin? Do you know the truth of its cessation? And the path to the cessation of suffering? But what does it matter if you do? Did you truly not weep; did you not suffer before the dynamite? What matter if the enlightened know such truths? The unenlightened dominate.

Beware the Book?
Beware the Iconoclasts.
Beware the Biblioclasts.

After having written a significant portion of his book *&* copious notes, Renato receives a letter from his brother full of masked fury, if not contempt. In quiet astonishment, as if stupefied by something improbable and astounding, he reads and rereads this letter, which states that his brother can no longer preserve his books *&* that, if Renato cannot soon remove them, he will donate them to an auction house. After a series of vituperative remarks and curses, the letter concludes with Renato's brother stating that, since he needs space, he will also have to dispose of Renato's bookshelves, that he will use them as firewood. "A baby is more important than the dusty refuse of a writer!"

*　　*　　*　　*　　*

The alignment of certain events, situations, and possibilities, often coinciding to the day or hour, endowed Renato's decisions with a sense of aptness, giving him no reason to question his choices. Yet he could not help but think that leaving New York and closing his apartment was rash, since it led to crises, breakdowns, and catastrophes. It is not that there were no beneficial things, triumphs and achievements of different kinds, but to have such a precarious existence at such a late age, to own nothing but books, to be essentially homeless, too destitute to regain one's things... For too long, Renato made hasty, whimsical decisions, without thought for the future, trusting that the ground beneath his feet would eventually grow more solid. Yet, perhaps such disasters are necessary, not negative, but a test of one's resolve; the work of a greater transformation whose outcome is not yet visible, just as the disasters were not before visible to him. *Is it not a ritual transformation that he is undergoing, the shedding of an old life, the anguish of the human-snake? Is it not an initiatory ordeal?* The state of living-death does not however enable him to think of life, to foresee the new life in formation, the transformation of his mode of being.

*　　*　　*　　*　　*

The strength I recently felt has faded. Unease rules. Disturbances. It is very difficult to work, to maintain sanity with such continuous instability. The threat of losing my library, the gesture itself… an unspeakable event. I feel gutted and listless, as if the simplest of things is impossible.

*   *   *   *   *

A friend writes to reassure Renato that his fracturing is not total nor ab-solute, noting that she herself recently underwent a similar crisis, was without any center, had no sense of self or direction, and thinking was impossible. I pivoted though from feeling extremely isolated and under threat of ostracization to feeling a sense of deluded harmony with every-one, and an absurd gratefulness for this harmony. What oscillating, un-steady creatures we are. How changeable, how fragile… and yet, if we can just hold on, wait out the storms, not do anything too drastic, we will find we have gotten through to another place… at least I hope that happens for you and that you are not truly in the grip of something more serious & life-threatening.

*   *   *   *   *

I have had two restoring days but everything remains too impermanent, volatile, in the chemical sense, to speak of any reliably stable progress. I am doubtful of there being no risk, for collapses occur, and permanent losses occur, radical *negative mutations* occur. Monstrosity. Death comes unexpectedly, as after any form of brain damage, we go through muta-tions. It is the death of one who used to be, and it can occur instanta-neously. The destruction of a former self. Our desolation may end in an ascent to higher places, by which nothing transcendent is meant, but a state of tranquility and oblivion, or into more menacing forms of silence, the result of explosions, of the most extreme form of shattering, of an ecstatic jubilation that results in psychic sparagmos. This dread seethes within us.

*   *   *   *   *

314

There have been too many 'revolutions,' too many overturnings. The spiraling has returned, the mental kaleidoscope, the fragmentation. *Fracturing* ... There are moments when I simply can't function, am paralyzed, numb. Either the world kills us, or we kill the world. Those whom the gods wish to destroy they first make mad. I'll break my staff, bury it certain fathoms in the earth, and deeper than did ever plummet sound I'll drown my book. *Solemn music!*

*　　*　　*　　*　　*

On January 3, several weeks after having auctioned off Renato's library, his brother hacks his bookcases into pieces & burns them in his fireplace, an act that he commits with gleeful but subdued fury, giving rise to a sense of relief & freedom.

*　　*　　*　　*　　*

*　　*　　*　　*　　*

The next day, the charred remains of a body are discovered on Nerval's grave. The identity of the person could not be verified, but the caretaker of the graveyard found a manuscript, unsigned, partially burnt, bearing the title:

Toward a Genealogy of the Sublime

*   *   *   *   *

I break open stars & find nothing, and again nothing, & then a word
in a foreign tongue.

Elisabeth Borchers

PROHIBITION!

"The organizational committee of the Union of Soviet Composers followed a fundamentally wrong line in the field of Soviet music. Instead of developing Soviet music in the spirit of socialist realism, ideinost' and narodnost', and to perfect the artistic mastery of Soviet composers, the organizational committee turned into a breeding-ground of formalist, anti-*narod* direction in Soviet music, which seriously damaged its development & has been condemned by the Party. The organizational committee not only failed to facilitate the development of creative discussion, of criticism and self-criticism among Soviet composers, but, on the contrary, it cultivated morals, alien to Soviet society, of suppression of criticism & self-criticism and promoted an unrestrained eulogizing of the creations of a small group of composers to cultivate friendly relations."

The Politburo Resolution

And so, in 2001, in Egypt, by order of Islamic Fundamentalists, the Egyptian Ministry of Culture burns 6,000 volumes of homoerotic poetry by 8th-C poet Abu Nuwas.

Beware the Book?

Beware Desire?

Beware Eroticism?

Beware the Neo-Fascists; beware the Bibliophobes.

As the cryptic gesture of the RPF is reported around the globe, radio, television, & internet broadcasts are also interrupted, signals intermittently short-circuiting, with poetry in different languages washing over, altering, or mutating each broadcast.

Commercials, congressional & presidential speeches, and other, similar forms of rhetoric are also short-circuited, disrupted, & mutated, sometimes broken with lengthy, extended silences.

The complete *world erasure* of all signage; a radical, pervasive palimpsest occurring simultaneously; a total blackening, erasing all slogans, all empty rhetoric, as if they were being engulfed and obliterated by dark matter itself.

And so, on March 5, 2001, in league with the Vishwa Hindu Parishad, Hindu Fundamentalist Activists burn copies of the Qur'an in New Delhi in protest against the destruction of the Bamiyan Buddhas.

What of the noble truths?

Beware the Book?

Beware Vengeance.

PROHIBITION!

"To write poetry after Auschwitz is barbaric."

"A perennial suffering has just as much right to find expression as a victim of torture has to scream. For this reason it *may* have been wrong to write that after Auschwitz poetry could no longer be written."

Adorno

El sueño de la razon produce monstruos.

Marsyas the *contra naturam*: not human, not animal, but indeterminate —
a disquieting, threatening, feral figure that others might call ... *degenerate*.
He who strives for the *nitimur in vetitum*.

An artist of contagion; an artist of the grotesque who fears not chaos
or formlessness, who fears not abstraction; an artist of deformation
— Marsyas boldly takes up the aulos, the instrument which distorted
Athena's ever-beautiful face, which deformed it, for he knows that art is
greater than beauty, & that beauty alone is not the sole province of art;
that art, too, must be questioned.

And so Marsyas howled, shrieking like a gorgon:

Quid me mihi detrahis?

The work of Marsyas is also the work of *amorphon*: the literature of the
unword; the painting of abstraction; the music of discord & dissonance.
That which is withdrawn and separate from material objects and practi-
cal matters; that which is *godcund*. The work of depersonification; the
erasure of the self — the deformed face is the deformed mask, the altered
persona, the metamorphosis on behalf of art; the proud fool: the *fol*, the
follis — the *folles*!

To move beyond logos, to move beyond mimesis, to move beyond the
classical — the disorienting melody, the disruptive image, the destabiliz-
ing word. The work of the *Amorphonists* is the work of true genesis; it
does not borrow objects from the real world; it creates its own. It reveals
the will of the artist. It is pure creation.

The pleasant taking leave of all sobriety is the work of the *Amorphonists*
who transport us into *Unheimlich* states, who invert & disrupt, who pro-
voke the feast & the festival, who open the realm of exuberance & frenetic
pleasure, who begin ... the *secret rites*. Do you not hear the death of Me-
dusa in this music? Do you not hear the shrieks of the gorgons? Marsyas,

he who recovers the lost or discarded art of *Amorphon*, the original *Entartete Künstler*, the ancestor of all *Entartete Künstlerin*. Have those who are *Entartete* truly fallen from their ancestry then?

Quid me mihi detrahis?

Beardless, civil, laurel-crowned, Apollo coolly brandishes his bone-handled knife as he inverts Marsyas, just as he inverted his lyre, reducing the satyr into an object of mockery upon which he plays, turning his body into an instrument of torture. The human animal must be dissected for the sake of knowledge, to know what an *Entartete* is. Gently, Apollo presses the blade into the skin of Marsyas, the *scorticoti*, violating the *amorphon* with ease.

Quid me mihi detrahis?

Devoid of emotion, *hulling* the satyr of his skin as if the act was a game, an experiment, Apollo exposes the subcutaneous echelons of the body, sounding its inner bands:

> griesly bloud spins from every part,
> sinewes lay discovered to the eye,
> quivering, skinless veynes lay nakedly beating,
> bowels pant in the bulk of a cavity,
> testicles & penis hang like meat in a butcher's stall,
> tendons, ligaments & sinew
> become but shere small strings,
> the new lyre upon which Apollo plays

This song denudes Marsyas of 16% of the weight of his body. Apollo calculates his every deed with exactitude; catalogs every action with the banality of an accountant. Hung in a cave like a leather jacket, the wind blows through the skin as if it were an aulos, a *follis*.

Quid me mihi detrahis?

Like Athena's deformed face, the body of Marsyas is deformed in this sac-
rifice & execution. Like Athena, Marsyas denounces the aulos, but only
because he is tortured, not because he could not stand to be a fool. In
this, are they not wed? Is Apollo's deformation of Marsyas not also a de-
formation of Athena, an expression of his desire to skin alive that chaste,
virginal harridan?

Blood & tears make up a river; pulverized bones, too; each part of an
ecology of catastrophe; a cycle of disaster.

If to abstract is to drag away, to detach, to pull apart, was not Apollo an
Amorphonist? Did he not become an *Entartete Künstler*, yet, in the service
of death?

The *Unzeitgemäße,*
    those who, thru s/~   \p~l~i/ ~t\ ~t/ ~in/ ~g/

        TRANSFORM TIME

          thru their
        f us-ION   s

t   r   a   c   i   n   g   ALL   of   h   i   s   t   o   r   y

          like Senecan figures
        they   map   T   I   M   E

       by way of the pressures of their age
     track the darkness of the present
as it casts its shadow on the past
                          a TOUCH
             which   a w a k e n s
and brings forward TIME
          till it activates
          the darkness

of the   N   O   W

Books melt like chunks of ice brought into a room. Everything grows smaller. Everything seems to me a book. Where is the difference between a book and a thing? I do not know life…

Everything grows smaller. Everything melts. Even Goethe melts. Brief time is allotted us. As it slips away, the hilt of that bloodless, brittle sword, broken off at the drainpipe one freezing day, chills the palm.

But thought — like the hangman steel of the "Nurmis" skates, which once skimmed along the blue, pimply ice — has not been blunted.

It is more & more difficult to turn the pages of the frozen book, bound in axes by the light of gas lanterns.

You, wood yards — black libraries of the city — we shall yet read, we shall still have a look.

Destroy your manuscript, but save whatever you have inscribed in the margin out of boredom, out of helplessness, and, as it were, in a dream. These secondary & involuntary creations of your fantasy will not be lost in the world…

Osip Mandelstam

Arbeit Macht Frei?

AND DURING HER NOCTURNAL REVELS,

JULIA CROWNS MARSYAS WITH FLOWERS

And so, during the 2003 Iraq War, the Iraq National Library and
Archive, the Al-Awqaf Library, the Central Library of the University of
Baghdad, the Library of Bayt al-Hikma, the Central Library of the Uni-
versity of Mosul, and other libraries are looted, set on fire, damaged, &
destroyed.

Beware the Book?

Beware the Publicum; beware the rabble

Beware the Plebiscite & the Mob, the terrible wielders of *bundles*.

Carte
Ethnographique
de
L'Europe

As investigators continue to be riddled by what they refer to as the "world-wide global conspiracy of RPF," an explosion of color manifests everywhere thru-out the world: lasers, projections of different kinds, light boxes, globes, & other forms of pure light:

The electric prose of incandescent color, a kaleidoscope of hues flashing at stroboscopic rhythms, a *light monument* to poiesis, blinking with intensity, then turning again to

He who sets out to write a book with a hunger for words, with a love of words, and with the vanity of words, in the language of yesterday or of today or of tomorrow, in the congealed language of a certain & firm step, he cannot undertake the task of liberation from language. I must destroy language within me, in front of me, & behind me step for step if I want to ascend in the critique of language, which is the most pressing task for thinking man; I must shatter each rung of the ladder by stepping upon it. He who wishes to follow me must reconstitute the rungs in order to shatter them once again.

Fritz Mauthner

And so, in 2014, *and now*, ISIS burns book after book, destroying the Libraries of Mosul University, the Libraries of the Anbar Province, private libraries, the Central Public Library in Ninawa, incinerating over 8,000 rare old books *&* manuscripts, Syriac books, Ottoman Empire books, and Iraqi newspapers.

Beware the Book? Beware the *klasmos* of Medieval Neo-Fascists.

Do they not know that every act of destruction is a form of self-destruction? When we are ready to kill for our beliefs, we must shatter our beliefs instead — *that is the greatest sacrifice that a 'believer' can make, the most noble.*

Death to Reverence. Death to Piety!

Let us laugh at the great masters of virtue and saints and poets *&* world-redeemers!

Let us learn to laugh at ourselves, as one has to laugh, for laughter is holy!

Shatter, shatter the good *&* the righteous!

Shatter!

after which each billboard & screen is

Arbeit Macht Frei?

AU-DESSUS ET EN DEHORS DES PAPYRUS,

IL Y A DES FORCES...

REVOLUTIONARY POETIC FRONT

MANUSCRIPTS DON'T BURN

FACE LIBER   ΠΟΙΗΣΗΣ AZAD
RIR   يخلق الحرّ   ΠΟΙΗΣΗΣ   ARB
CHT FREI   ΠΟΙΗΣΗΣ MAKES FR
ΟΙΗΣΗΣ ΚΑΝΕΙ ΔΩΡΕΑΝ   ΠΟΙΗ
PAR LA ΠΟΙΗΣΗΣ   A ΠΟΙΗΣΗΣ
FACE LIBER   ΠΟΙΗΣΗΣ AZAD M
RIR   يخلق الحرّ   ΠΟΙΗΣΗΣ   ARB
HT FREI   ΠΟΙΗΣΗΣ MAK   FR
ΙΗΣΗΣ ΚΑΝΕΙ ΔΩΡΕΑΝ
PAR LA ΠΟΙΗΣΗΣ   A ΠΟ
ACE LIBER   ΠΟΙΗΣΗΣ AZAD
RIR   يخلق الحرّ   ΠΟΙΗΣΗΣ   ARB
CHT FREI   ΠΟΙΗΣΗΣ MAKES FR
ΟΙΗΣΗΣ ΚΑΝΕΙ ΔΩΡΕΑΝ   ΠΟΙΗ
AR LA ΠΟΙΗΣΗΣ   A ΠΟΙΗΣΗΣ

ISAZAD ΠΟΙΗΣΗΣ ÖZ
IT MACHT FREI ?
EE   ΠΟΙΗΣΗ
ΣΗΣ RENDE
SZABADD
ISAZAD
T MACHT FRE
E ΠΟΙ
RE
LIBER
ΣΗΣ TE
SAZA   ΠΟΙΗΣΗΣ SZGÜRLES
IT MACHT FREI ? ΠΟΙΗΣΗΣ M
E   ΠΟΙΗΣΗΣ HACE LIBRES   Π
ΣΗΣ RENDE LIBERI LA LIBERTÉ
SZABADDA TÉSZ ΠΟΙΗΣΗΣ TÉ

COLOPHON

SHATTERING THE MUSES

was typeset in InDesign cc

The text and page numbers are set in *Adobe Jenson Pro*

The copy in blackletter is set in *Baſtarda* and *Old London*

Book design & typesetting: Alessandro Segalini

Cover design: Rainer J. Hanshe & Alessandro Segalini

Cover image: *Gutenberg (version 1)* © 2016 Federico Gori

SHATTERING THE MUSES

is published by Contra Mundum Press.

Its printer has received Chain of Custody certification from:

The Forest Stewardship Council,

The Programme for the Endorsement of Forest Certification,

& The Sustainable Forestry Initiative.

Contra Mundum Press   New York · London · Melbourne

ORIGINAL WORKS BY FEDERICO GORI

Cover: *Gutenberg (version 1).* Ink and enamel on aluminum, 19 x 25 cm, 2015/2016.

8: *Calliope (version 1).* Ink and enamel on aluminum, 19 x 25 cm, 2015/2016.

9: *Clio (version 1).* Ink and enamel on aluminum, 19 x 25 cm, 2015/2016.

10: *Euterpe (version 1).* Ink and enamel on aluminum, 19 x 25 cm, 2015/2016.

11: *Erato (version 2).* Ink and enamel on aluminum, 19 x 25 cm, 2015/2016.

12: *Melpomene (version 1).* Ink and enamel on aluminum, 19 x 25 cm, 2015/2016.

13: *Polyhymnia (version 1).* Ink and enamel on aluminum, 19 x 25 cm, 2015/2016.

14: *Terpsichore (version 1).* Ink and enamel on aluminum, 19 x 25 cm, 2015/2016.

15: *Thalia (version 1).* Ink and enamel on aluminum, 19 x 25 cm, 2015/2016.

16: *Urania.* Ink and enamel on aluminum, 19 x 25 cm, 2015/2016.

18: *Martin Luther's Birthday.* Ink and enamel on aluminum, 19 x 25 cm, 2015/2016.

23/24: *Lost but not Forgotten (version 1).* Ink and enamel on aluminum, 38 x 25 cm, 2015/2016.

36: *One Day I'm Going to Grow Wings (#1).* Ink and enamel on aluminum, 19 x 25 cm, 2015/2016.

55: *Concentration Camp.* Ink and enamel on aluminum, 19 x 25 cm, 2015/2016.

77: *Marsyas (version 1).* Ink and enamel on aluminum, 19 x 25 cm, 2015/2016.

78: *River (detail).* Ink and enamel on aluminum, 38 x 25 cm, 2015/2016.

81/82: *Lost but not Forgotten (version 2).* Ink and enamel on aluminum, 38 x 25 cm, 2015/2016.

133: *Marsyas (version 2).* Ink and enamel on aluminum, 19 x 25 cm, 2015/2016.

134: *River (detail).* Ink and enamel on aluminum, 38 x 25 cm, 2015/2016.

142: *Squealing Monkey.* Ink and enamel on aluminum, 19 x 25 cm, 2015/2016.

163: *Marsyas (version 3).* Ink and enamel on aluminum, 19 x 25 cm, 2015/2016.

164: *River (detail).* Ink and enamel on aluminum, 38 x 25 cm, 2015/2016.

167/168: *Lost but not Forgotten (version 3).* Ink and enamel on aluminum, 38 x 25 cm, 2015/2016.

175: *Revolutionary Poetic Front (version 1).* Ink and enamel on aluminum, 19 x 25 cm, 2015/2016.

177: *Calliope (version 2).* Ink and enamel on aluminum, 19 x 25 cm, 2015/2016.

178: *Clio (version 1).* Ink and enamel on aluminum, 19 x 25 cm, 2015/2016.

179: *Euterpe (version 2).* Ink and enamel on aluminum, 19 x 25 cm, 2015/2016.

194: *Marsyas (version 4).* Ink and enamel on aluminum, 19 x 25 cm, 2015/2016.

195/196: *River.* Ink and enamel on aluminum, 38 x 25 cm, 2015/2016.

234: *Gutenberg (version 1).* Ink and enamel on aluminum, 19 x 25 cm, 2015/2016.

272: *The Tower.* Ink and enamel on aluminum, 19 x 25 cm, 2015/2016.

274: *Corteccia (#1).* Coal and ash on canvas, 175 x 175 cm, 2015.

275: *Corteccia (#2).* Coal and ash on canvas, 175 x 175 cm, 2015.

276: *Corteccia (#3).* Coal and ash on canvas, 175 x 175 cm, 2015.

277: *Corteccia (#4).* Coal and ash on canvas, 175 x 175 cm, 2015.

278: *Corteccia (#5).* Coal and ash on canvas, 175 x 175 cm, 2015.

279: *Corteccia (#6).* Coal and ash on canvas, 175 x 175 cm, 2015.

283: *Revolutionary Poetic Front (version 2).* Ink and enamel on aluminum, 19 x 25 cm, 2015/2016.

296: *River (detail).* Ink and enamel on aluminum, 38 x 25 cm, 2015/2016.

298: *One Day I'm Going to Grow Wings (#2).* Ink and enamel on aluminum, 19 x 25 cm, 2015/2016.

331/332: *Lost but not Forgotten (version 4).* Ink and enamel on aluminum, 38 x 25 cm, 2015/2016.

341: *Revolutionary Poetic Front (version 3).* Ink and enamel on aluminum, 19 x 25 cm, 2015/2016.

343/344: *Poiesis.* Ink and enamel on aluminum, 38 x 25 cm, 2015/2016.

CONTRA MUNDUM PRESS

Dedicated to the value & the indispensable importance of the individual voice, to works that test the boundaries of thought & experience.

The primary aim of Contra Mundum is to publish translations of writers who in their use of form and style are *à rebours*, or who deviate significantly from more programmatic & spurious forms of experimentation. Such writing attests to the volatile nature of modernism. Our preference is for works that have not yet been translated into English, are out of print, or are poorly translated, for writers whose thinking & æsthetics are in opposition to timely or mainstream currents of thought, value systems, or moralities. We also reprint obscure and out-of-print works we consider significant but which have been forgotten, neglected, or overshadowed.

There are many works of fundamental significance to *Weltliteratur* (*& Weltkultur*) that still remain in relative oblivion, works that alter and disrupt standard circuits of thought — these warrant being encountered by the world at large. It is our aim to render them more visible.

For the complete list of forthcoming publications, please visit our website. To be added to our mailing list, send your name & email address to: info@contramundum.net

Contra Mundum Press
P.O. Box 1326
New York, NY 10276
USA

OTHER CONTRA MUNDUM PRESS TITLES

Gilgamesh
Ghérasim Luca, *Self-Shadowing Prey*
Rainer J. Hanshe, *The Abdication*
Walter Jackson Bate, *Negative Capability*
Miklós Szentkuthy, *Marginalia on Casanova*
Fernando Pessoa, *Philosophical Essays*
Elio Petri, *Writings on Cinema & Life*
Friedrich Nietzsche, *The Greek Music Drama*
Richard Foreman, *Plays with Films*
Louis-Auguste Blanqui, *Eternity by the Stars*
Miklós Szentkuthy, *Towards the One & Only Metaphor*
Josef Winkler, *When the Time Comes*
William Wordsworth, *Fragments*
Josef Winkler, *Natura Morta*
Fernando Pessoa, *The Transformation Book*
Emilio Villa, *The Selected Poetry of Emilio Villa*
Robert Kelly, *A Voice Full of Cities*
Pier Paolo Pasolini, *The Divine Mimesis*
Miklós Szentkuthy, *Prae, Vol. 1*
Federico Fellini, *Making a Film*
Robert Musil, *Thought Flights*
Sándor Tar, *Our Street*
Lorand Gaspar, *Earth Absolute*
Josef Winkler, *The Graveyard of Bitter Oranges*
Ferit Edgü, *Noone*
Jean-Jacques Rousseau, *Narcissus*
Ahmad Shamlu, *Born Upon the Dark Spear*
Jean-Luc Godard, *Phrases*
Otto Dix, *Letters, Vol. 1*
Maura Del Serra, *Ladder of Oaths*
Pierre Senges, *The Major Refutation*
Charles Baudelaire, *My Heart Laid Bare & Other Texts*
Joseph Kessel, *Army of Shadows*

SOME FORTHCOMING TITLES

Pierre Senges, *Ahab*
Gerard Depardieu, *Innocent*

ABOUT THE AUTHORS

Rainer J. Hanshe is a writer. He is the author of two novels, *The Acolytes* (2010) and *The Abdication* (2012), and a hybrid text created in collaboration with Federico Gori, *Shattering the Muses* (2017). His second novel, *The Abdication*, has been translated into Slovakian (2015), Italian (2016), and Turkish (2017). He is the editor of Richard Foreman's *Plays with Films* (2013) and Wordsworth's *Fragments* (2014), and the translator of Baudelaire's *My Heart Laid Bare & Other Texts* (2017) and Joseph Kessel's *Army of Shadows*. Hanshe has also written numerous essays on Nietzsche, principally concerning synesthesia, incubation, and agonism. He is the founder of Contra Mundum Press and *Hyperion: On the Future of Æsthetics*. Other work of his has appeared in *Sinn und Form, Jelenkor*, ChrisMarker.org, *Asymptote, Quarterly Conversation, Black Sun Lit*, and elsewhere. Hanshe is currently working on two novels, *Humanimality*, and *Now, Wonder*, and *In Praise of Dogs*, a photojournalism project with Harald Hutter.

Federico Gori, who was born in Prato in 1977, currently lives and works in Pistoia. After studying painting at the Accademia di Belle Arti in Florence, he was invited to show his work in Prato's Palazzo del Comune in 2002 in the context of an event entitled *Gemine Muse*, which was devoted to displaying the work of young artists in the museums of Europe. He was awarded a resident stage in 2003 by the Fondazione "Il Giardino di Daniel Spœrri. Hic Terminus Hæret," where he produced a site-specific work for display in the park. The exhibitions in which he has taken part in recent years include: 54th *Biennale di Venezia*, Padiglione Accademie, Venezia, 2011; *Di fragilità e potenza*, Palazzo Strozzi, Firenze, 2013; *Talent Prize* 2013, where he won the Special Award "Metaenergia," Casa dell'Architettura, Roma, 2013; *Come Afferrare il Vento*, Museo Palazzo Fabroni Arti Visive Contemporanee, Pistoia, 2015; *Colorful*, Sifang Art Museum, Nanjing, Jiangsu P.R.China, 2015; *Governare il caso, L'opera nel suo farsi dagli anni sessanta ai nostri giorni*, Pinacoteca Comunale di Città di Castello, Perugia, 2015; *Rebuilding the Future*, Rossana Maiorca Cycle Route, Siracusa, 2015; and *Underground #2*, Museo Palazzo Fabroni Arti Visive Contemporanee, Pistoia 2016. In 2017, he was an Artist in Residence at La Panaceé, Centre d'Art Contemporain, Montpellier, France, invited by Le Bureau des Arts & Territoires for the European Project The Spur ETACEC 16–18.

www.ingramcontent.com/pod-product-compliance
Lightning Source LLC
Chambersburg PA
CBHW041207100726
47911CB00017B/884